A BAKER'S FIELD GUIDE TO
Chocolate Chip
Cookies

DEDE WILSON

THE HARVARD COMMON PRESS

Boston, Massachusetts

THE HARVARD COMMON PRESS
535 Albany Street
Boston, Massachusetts 02118
www.harvardcommonpress.com

NESTLÉ® and TOLL HOUSE® are registered trademarks of
Societé des Produits Nestlé S.A., Vevey, Switzerland.

Printed in China
Printed on acid-free paper

The Library of Congress has cataloged the original edition as follows:

Wilson, Dede.
  A baker's field guide to chocolate chip cookies / Dede Wilson.
      p. cm.
  Includes index.
  ISBN 1-55832-295-7 (concealed wire-o : alk. paper)
      1. Cookies. I. Title.
  TX772.W523 2004
  641.8'654—dc22

                                                              2004003312

Reprint ISBN: 978-1-55832-750-4 (pbk.)

Special bulk-order discounts are available on this and other Harvard
Common Press books. Companies and organizations may purchase
books for premiums or resale, or may arrange a custom edition, by
contacting the Marketing Director at the address above.

Book design by Night & Day Design
Cover and interior photographs by Eric Roth Photography
Cookie preparation and styling by Mary Bandereck

10 9 8 7 6 5 4 3 2 1

David, thank you for your

ever present support. I wouldn't be

where I am today without you.

And to Marion Dussault—the Oh

So Minty, Oh So Chocolatey Creamy

Dream Bars are for you.

Thank you for being such a

great friend.

Contents

Acknowledgments

First of all, let me say that without Ruth Wakefield and her original Toll House cookie recipe, this book would not have been possible. Would someone else have come up with her idea? Perhaps, but she goes down in history as the mother of all chocolate chip cookies. The Nestlé company was smart enough to jump on the bandwagon early and manufacture the perfect size chocolate morsel for her "new" cookie and print her original recipe right on the label, where it remains today. My thanks also go to the current folks at Nestlé, specifically Roz Ohearn, who kept me swimming in morsels while testing these recipes. I particularly love the new chunk style!

When I wrote my first book, a new world opened up to me—one of agents and editors, publishers, designers, photographers, food stylists, prop stylists, and public relation specialists. Soon I became aware of those working hard behind the scene, like copy editors, line editors, special sales department and marketing folks, and many, many more. No book is truly written alone and as far as I am concerned, mine are far better off for it! I have been blessed with wonderful publishing professionals from the get-go. Here's how it works:

Maureen and Eric Lasher, my agents. They help me hone proposals, broker deals, feed me ideas, and care for me more than I could have ever expected.

Bruce Shaw, publisher. In this day and age of huge mega-conglomerate publishing houses, Bruce continues to run an intimate, quality "house." I love his hands-on way of running things and I feel like a part of The Harvard Common Press family. He, ultimately, was the one who okayed this book. Thank you!

Pam Hoenig, editor. Pam came up with the idea for a "field guide" format cookbook and sold her publisher on the concept with me at the helm.

The editing process is complex: thanks to Valerie Cimino, managing editor; Jodi Marchowsky, production editor; Virginia Downes, production manager; and Pat Jalbert-Levine, freelance project manager. A special thanks to Debra Hudak for her keen eye during the copyediting process. Everyone at The Harvard Common Press is so hands-on; the editing process is thorough and a joy.

Skye Stewart, marketing director. Skye gets the word out and keeps me busy. Whether it is a television appearance or a signing, she's got me covered.

Betsy Young, sales director. It's all about selling books and Betsy helped get my *A Baker's Field Guide to Christmas Cookies* out on the shelves in a big way. I know she will again with this one.

Thanks to Sunshine Erickson, trade marketing manager; Abbey Phalen, special sales manager; Dana Garczewski, marketing associate; Liza Beth, publicity associate; Megan Weireter, office manager. Simply put, Megan gets it all done. If a book has to get from the warehouse to a destination, she makes it happen.

Big, big thanks to Night and Day Design, Eric Roth for the photography, and Mary Bandereck, who made my cookies look scrumptious.

Juanita, Tom, Judy, and especially Daniel—a crew of serious recipe testers.

Pam and Jeff, hardcore dessert lovers. I'll call them up, invite them to sample a test cookie, and they'll jump on their bike and drive 30 minutes for the privilege— and bring their own plastic containers for extras! I love your enthusiasm.

Mary, Mary, Mary (McNamara, that is). What can I say? We are on a roll! I couldn't ask for a better baking accomplice.

Thanks to my dad, Moses Acosta, and friends, Linda Kielson and Amy Wasserman. You all claim to be president of my fan club. I don't want to demote any of you; could you share the position? I love you all.

Ravenna, Freeman, and Forrester, my cookie-eating kids.

David, my partner. He may not love cookies, but he loves me—good enough!

Introduction

Chocolate chip cookies are often the first cookies that Americans learn how to bake. In fact, it is often the very first anything that we learn how to make in the kitchen, period! And why not? They use basic ingredients and are easy and delicious. You can bake them crunchy or chewy, small or large, extra tiny or as large as pizzas. They also keep well, are perfect for bake sales, and you can vary the basic recipe endlessly. I don't think I have ever met anyone who doesn't like some sort of chocolate chip cookie, whether it's with nuts or without, crunchy or soft and gooey. Everyone has a favorite kind.

I love the classic Toll House chocolate chip cookie (see page 78), but this book is about bringing you the original recipe as well as opening up a world of chip-filled possibilities. If you like chocolate chips, you've come to the right place.

Every cookie in this book features chocolate chips of some sort in some way, whether it be white, milk, or dark chocolate chips, chunks, or tiny bits. You'll find drop cookies, bar cookies, and even fancy shaped and molded cookies. This book has it all in terms of the wide variety that exists in the cookie kingdom—they just all happen to have pieces of chocolate in them!

Most of these cookies are very easy to put together and are great to make with kids. Others are a tad more complex, but I am sure you will find the chocolate chip cookie of your dreams. I have to say, I have never had so much fun developing recipes. I am sure you will agree that chocolate chip cookies are as fun to make as they are delicious to eat. So let's stop chatting and get ourselves into the kitchen. Happy Baking!

How to Use This Book

This book is a companion book to my first "field guide" cookbook,

A Baker's Field Guide to Christmas Cookies. And, like that book, every

cookie here has its own page with the Type (such as drop, rolled, shaped,

or bar cookie, etc.), a Description (what you can expect to taste), and

Field Notes (where I give you tips and further information), as well as its

Lifespan (which gives storage information and how long you can expect

the cookie to stay fresh). For each cookie you will also find symbols for

special characteristics as listed in the chart on the following page.

KEY TO SYMBOLS

 dough freezes well

 cookies keep well

 fun to make with kids

 quick to make

 sturdy enough to mail

Ingredients

Here is a short list of frequently called for ingredients used in this book. If you start with high-quality ingredients, you'll get the best results.

BUTTER: Use fresh unsalted butter.

GRANULATED SUGAR: Use regular white granulated sugar.

Light and dark brown sugar: These should be packed into a measuring cup when measuring.

Confectioners' sugar: Also called powdered sugar, this almost always needs sifting before using.

Colored sugars: Colored sugars are used to decorate cookies and can be found in a variety of colors. See Resources for ordering information.

HONEY AND MOLASSES: Use mild-flavored orange blossom or wildflower honey and unsulfured molasses for these cookies. Both can be sticky—and tricky—to measure. Lightly coat the inside of your liquid measuring cup with nonstick cooking spray, then pour in the desired amount. It will then slip right out.

EGGS: Use eggs graded "large."

FLOUR: Use all-purpose flour. These recipes were tested with King Arthur Unbleached All-Purpose Flour.

LEAVENERS: Make sure your baking soda and baking powder are fresh.

SALT: Use table salt for these cookies.

MILK, CREAM CHEESE, AND SOUR CREAM: Use full-fat varieties.

HEAVY CREAM: Use cream labeled "heavy" as opposed to "whipping" for best results. The "heavy" has a higher butterfat content.

EXTRACTS: Use pure vanilla and almond extracts. I usually add extracts directly to the blended butter-sugar mixture, as I think the butter, or fat, disperses the extract flavor best at this stage. If the extract is added at a different stage, it is because the recipe source called for it that way.

CITRUS ZESTS: Make sure to use just the colored part of the zest and not the bitter white pith beneath.

NUTS: Make sure nuts are fresh with no rancid smell.

Equipment and Techniques

MEASURING CUPS AND SPOONS: For dry ingredients, I use high-quality stainless-steel cups that are sturdy enough not to dent (dents make for inaccurate measurements). The same goes for measuring

9

spoons. For liquid measurements, I use standard Pyrex measuring cups available at most supermarkets and kitchenware stores.

MIXER: I used a freestanding 5-quart KitchenAid mixer to test these recipes. If using a handheld mixer, the mixing times will be longer.

FOOD PROCESSOR: The recipes were tested with a KitchenAid 11-cup Ultra Power Food Processor fitted with a metal blade.

MICROWAVE OVEN: It is hard to standardize recipes using microwave ovens, as they come equipped with various wattage. Always follow your manufac-

A Baker's Field Guide to Chocolate

Hey folks, this is why we are all here! Morsels, chips, little bits of chocolate, chunks of chocolate, melted, grated, and chopped—all of these cookies feature chocolate, so it stands to reason that you should use the right kind. Some of the recipes call for morsels, or chips, and those are readily found in any supermarket. When a recipe suggests melting chocolate or requires finely chopped or grated chocolate, start with bulk chocolate that you cut to size to weigh or chop and measure. For chunks, you can chop bulk chocolate or Nestlé makes a semisweet chocolate chunk that you can pour right out of the bag. Scharffen Berger (for bittersweet), Callebaut (for milk and white chocolate), Valrhona (for semisweet and bittersweet), and Ghirardelli (for white chocolate) brands are my bulk choices. If a reference says "dark" chocolate, you can use either bittersweet or semisweet. If one or the other is specified, use what is suggested.

Chocolate "morsels" or chips: Most of these recipes use chocolate morsels, either white, milk, or semisweet. There are a number of brands now available on the market; choose the one that pleases you the most. When I say "chip" or "morsel"

throughout the book, you can consider the terms interchangeable and to mean a standard-sized chip. Some recipes call for miniature semisweet chocolate chips, which can be found right next to the other chips in the supermarket. I often use them where I still want chocolate in the dough, but in a finer texture than the larger chips would provide.

I tested these recipes with Nestlé chips. For their brand you can find packages of the standard-sized semisweet morsels in 6-ounce and 12-ounce bags, which measure 1 cup and 2 cups respectively. Nestlé also makes semisweet chocolate chunks, sold in an 11.5-ounce bag, which measures out to about 1¾ cups. Their miniature semisweet morsels and white morsels come in a 12-ounce size, the milk chocolate in 11.5-ounce bags, and the butterscotch in 11-ounce bags. For peanut butter chips, I used Reese's and those come in a 10-ounce bag. Because of this variation in bag sizes between types of chips and across brands, I call for the cup amount, or actual volume measurement, in the recipes, instead of saying "1 bag."

Chocolate chunks: For semisweet chunks, you can pick up a package of

turer's directions for specific information. I use the microwave to melt dark chocolate and butter. Start by microwaving on half (50 percent) power for short periods of time.

Many cookie sheets are flimsy, warp, and allow burning. These recipes were tested with heavyweight aluminum or rimmed cookie sheets (also called half-sheet pans

Nestlé's semisweet chocolate chunks (see page 10) or chop your own from bulk chocolate. For bittersweet, milk, or white chocolate chunks, I chop my own. The recipe will specify size, usually $\frac{1}{4}$- to $\frac{1}{2}$-inch chunks. For the recipes that call for $\frac{1}{8}$-inch pieces, it is okay to include slivers and shards.

Chopping chocolate: Some recipes call for chocolate chunks, others for finely chopped chocolate. Either way, start with a chunk of bulk chocolate, which can be found in specialty food stores or through mail order. Use a sharp knife and chop using the length of the knife until the desired size and texture is achieved. *Never, ever* insert the tip of your knife into a hunk of chocolate, because you will snap the tip right off. Believe me, I know from experience. Actually, it is pretty funny. My friend and recipe tester Mary McNamara and I have identical 8-inch chef's knives with snapped-off tips from back in the days when we were less experienced and more cavalier with our equipment. You can also buy something called a chocolate chipper (see Sweet Celebrations in Resources), which is like an ultra heavy-duty fork with strong tines. It works very well for making chunks.

When you chop bulk chocolate, you will most likely get pieces of all sizes to begin with, including slivers and shards. These do not belong in recipes calling for larger pieces (such as $\frac{1}{2}$-inch chunks), but they are perfect for recipes calling for $\frac{1}{8}$-inch pieces. Save those slivers and shards for this purpose, or use them for melting.

Melting chocolate: When the recipe calls for chocolate that is to be melted, be it white, milk, or dark, use bulk chocolate, not chips. Chips and morsels are formulated to keep their shape even when exposed to heat.

White chocolate: Look for white chocolate that lists cocoa butter in the ingredients and not palm or other oils. The cocoa butter will give it a chocolatey flavor and aroma.

Cocoa: These recipes call for Dutch-processed unsweetened cocoa powder, so check the label. It should say "Dutch-processed" or "alkalized," but if it says "natural," that's not the right kind. You can find Dutch-processed cocoa in the supermarket.

Black cocoa: This is a very dark cocoa available through King Arthur Flour The Baker's Catalogue. It gives your cookies a deep dark flavor and color similar to Oreos and is called for in one of the recipes in this book.

or jellyroll pans). Thinner sheets will more than likely brown cookies faster. But, and this is a big but, this is based on how these pans performed for me in my kitchen in my oven. Your oven might work symbiotically with another cookie-sheet pan even better, so it is really up to you to experiment. In general, however, the heavier the cookie sheet, the better for even baking. Try doubling up your cookie sheets if you find you are getting burned bottoms. There are insulated cookie sheets available, but they often prevent cookies from suitably browning, which I do not find desirable.

PARCHMENT PAPER: Parchment is available in rolls, like aluminum foil, from kitchenware stores and supermarkets. I use it to line my cookie sheets to eliminate sticking.

COOLING RACKS: Properly cooled baked goods will have the best texture and cooling racks are necessary to help diffuse heat efficiently from a pan hot from the oven.

BENCH SCRAPER: This is a rectangular piece of stainless steel with a wooden or hard plastic handle along one long side. I use it to gather ingredients together from my work surface, scrape up bits of dry ingredients, like chopped chocolate, spread batter into pans, and scrape my work surface clean after rolling out dough. But my favorite use is for cutting

bars cleanly (see page 14, Recipe Yields and Cutting Bars).

Forming Cookies and Ice Cream Scoops

For years I have read recipes that say "drop batter by teaspoonfuls" and when I took the time to think about it, I realized I had no idea what they meant. When I actually measured a teaspoonfull, it was much tinier than what was intended. When I took two teaspoons out of my utensil drawer (you know, the spoons you use to eat cereal with) and scooped up batter to drop on the cookie sheets, like most home bakers do, there was no uniformity or any way to really know how much batter I was doling out.

For these recipes to result in accurate baking times and yield counts, I wanted to be more precise in measuring. Many drop cookies end up being a generously rounded teaspoon in size and I found that an ice cream scoop (called a food disher) not only facilitates measuring, but allows quick scooping and dropping onto cookie sheets since it has a quick-release mechanism. If you want to duplicate my recipes as closely as possible, I suggest you get one of these. It is a Zeroll brand #100 scoop and is available through King Arthur Flour The Baker's Catalogue (see Resources). It will make many of these recipes go very quickly and the tool is very easy to use. To use an ice cream scoop effectively for

Good Cookie Tip

A cookie scoop helps compact the dough as it is measured out, which helps cookies retain their shape during baking.

forming cookies, dip the scoop into the batter, generously filling the bowl of the scoop. Scrape off the excess batter against the sides of the bowl to form a level scoop, then drop directly onto cookie sheet. Some of the recipes call for a generously rounded tablespoon and that measurement can be doled out with a Zeroll #40 scoop.

If a stiff batter is to be rolled into a ball between your palms, I give you specific measurements and directions such as "roll dough between your palms into 1-inch balls." Actually measure the first cookie with a ruler, then you can roll the rest by eye.

When rolling out dough to cut with cookie cutters, there will be a thickness given, such as ¼ inch. It is a good idea to actually measure the thickness of the dough for accurate results.

Freezing Dough

Some cookie dough freezes well. To know which cookie dough can be frozen, look for the "dough freezes well" icon 🌡. Then, at the stage in the recipe where the dough requires chilling, double wrap the dough in plastic wrap, slip it into a heavy-duty zipper-lock bag, remove all the air, and freeze up to a month. Defrost the dough in the refrigerator overnight, then proceed with the recipe.

Good Cookie Tip

My recipes will say "drop by generously rounded teaspoon." The exact measurement is supposed to be about 1¾ teaspoons. Feel free to scoop and drop batter any way you like, but actually measure out the first cookie so that you will then know how to measure out the rest by eye. Remember, if you use a different amount, your baking times, yield, and results will vary from those stated in the recipe. Same goes for recipes that say "drop by generously rounded tablespoon" in which the measurement is about 1½ tablespoonfuls.

Baking Times

Simply put, baking times are approximate and that is why every recipe says, "bake about" a certain number of minutes. A visual description of the cookie when it is done is also given. The simple fact is that your oven might have hot spots and/or your cookie sheets might perform differently than mine, so always check for doneness before the suggested baking time—and use the visual cues that are provided in every recipe—they always take precedence over baking times.

Number of Pans in Oven

Cookies need to have an even flow of heat and air all around them to bake as evenly and beautifully as possible. This is partially accomplished by spacing the cookies on the sheets as directed in individual recipes, but another important technique is to limit the number of pans in the oven at any given time. While most ovens have at least three racks, I find that baking one or two pans at a time gives the best results and that is how I tested these recipes. If you crowd the oven, you might burn your cookies or, at the very least, get different and unexpected results. Because of this approach, the recipes call for a maximum of two cookie-sheet pans; you will need to reuse your pans a few times for most recipes. Always let pans cool before reusing.

ROTATING PANS HALFWAY THROUGH BAKING: To help your cookies to bake as evenly as possible, another technique is to rotate pans front to back (and even between racks) in the oven at least once during baking.

Proper Cooling

You might think the recipe is over once the cookies are out of the oven, but proper cooling is essential for a great final result. Some cookies will initially be cooled still on the pan set on a rack for a few moments before being transferred to the rack directly to cool completely. Others are removed from the pan immediately to instantly stop residual cooking from the remaining heat of the pan. Follow the specific instructions given in a particular recipe. And always cool completely before placing cookies in storage containers to prevent condensation from forming.

Recipe Yields and Cutting Bars

Each recipes has a "yield" number, which tells you how many cookies or bars you will get, if you follow my directions. For cookies that are rolled out, I tell you what size cookie cutter I use and the yield will say "fifty 3-inch

cookies." Perhaps you want to use a cookie cutter of a different size. That's fine, but know that your yield will be different, as will your baking time.

For bars, the recipe will say "Cut into 16 bars (4 x 4)." This means that you divide the pan into horizontal rows of 4 bars by vertical rows of 4 bars to give you the suggested 16 bars. Bars can often be cut smaller or larger, which will alter your yield.

To cut bars, I definitely have a preferred method using a bench scraper (see page 12 for a more detailed description of this tool). Take it by the handle and press the sharp edge straight down into the bars; repeat to make a complete cut either across or down the length of the pan by lifting and pressing, lifting and pressing. If the bars are sticky, wipe the blade clean between cuts with a wet, warm cloth. Cutting in this fashion eliminates the bulk of the drag created by pulling a knife through a pan of bars; the edges of your bars will be cleaner and give you prettier results.

Tempering Chocolate for Dipping Cookies

Some of the cookies in the book call for a dip in melted chocolate after cooling, such as the Ginger Chip Brown Sugar Shortbread Fingers on page 102. If the chocolate is tempered, which simply means to melt it in a particular way, the results will be very professional looking. Tempered chocolate will stay glossy even without refrigeration and adds a polished look to your cookies. This is accomplished by a careful melting procedure, which stabilizes the fat crystals in the cocoa butter, and prevents the chocolate from streaking after cooling. To quick-temper chocolate:

- Start with the desired amount of chocolate as stated in the recipe and chop it very finely.
- Place about two-thirds of it in the top of a double boiler set over gently simmering water.
- Stir gently to encourage melting, but not vigorously, which will add air.
- As soon as the chocolate is melted, remove it from the heat and wipe the bottom of the pot to eliminate any chances of water droplets reaching the chocolate, which would cause it to seize. (You'll know if it has seized because it will become overly thickened and grainy.)
- Add about one-third of the remaining chopped chocolate and stir gently. The residual heat will melt it.
- As soon as it is melted, add the remaining chocolate in two more stages, continuing to stir gently until it is completely melted.

It should now be ready to use. To double check whether it is ready, dip your index finger into the chocolate and place a dab of melted chocolate on your lower lip; it should feel barely warm, but not hot. If it is too hot, stir in some more chopped chocolate. If you have an instant-read thermometer, place it into the chocolate and it should read between 89 and 91 degrees (for dark chocolate, which is the only type tempered and used in this book).

Please note that it is easiest to temper at least 8 ounces of chocolate, but some of the recipes call for less. The amount listed in the recipe is the amount you need for that specific recipe; here is what I suggest. If you are baking two or more cookies that require tempered chocolate, consider making them on the same day so that you can temper one batch of chocolate, which will make your cookie baking process very efficient. Otherwise, consider tempering at least 8 ounces and any unused chocolate can be allowed to harden; then you can chop it up and add it to any cookie that uses dark chocolate morsels or chunks, or fold it into ice cream.

Peeling and Toasting Nuts

HAZELNUTS: One technique will both skin and toast hazelnuts. Spread nuts in a single layer on a cookie sheet and bake in a preheated 350°F oven until they begin to give off an aroma and the skins have turned dark brown and have split, exposing the browning nut. This will take about 12 minutes. Shake the pan once or twice during toasting to encourage even browning.

Remove from the oven and let cool on a rack, then take clean kitchen towels and rub the nuts vigorously between them. With a little work, the skins will come off. My hazelnuts usually retain a tiny bit of skin on them; that's fine. Hazelnuts can be purchased peeled, at an added expense.

ALMONDS: Almonds are sold whole (either blanched or natural), sliced (blanched or natural), and slivered (blanched). If you care to spend the extra money on whole blanched almonds, go ahead; I often do as it saves time. If you want or need to peel whole ones yourself, follow these instructions. Drop them in boiling water and blanch for 1 minute, then drain. Once they're cool enough to handle, you should be able to slip the skins right off with your fingers. To toast almonds, spread them in a single layer on a cookie sheet and bake in a preheated 350°F oven until they begin to give off an aroma and are a light golden brown color. This will take 5 to 10 minutes, depending on the amount of nuts and whether they are whole, slivered, or sliced. Shake the pan once or twice during toasting to encourage even browning. Remove from the oven and let cool on a rack before using in a recipe.

Walnuts, pecans, pistachios, and macadamias do not need to be peeled. To toast, follow directions as described above for almonds. The timing will vary depending on the quantity of nuts on the pan as well as the type (size) of nut.

Always cool nuts before chopping them. The oils, which will have been brought to the surface by the heat, must be reabsorbed or the nuts could turn greasy when chopped.

Storing Cookies

Cookies, whether soft, chewy, or crisp, will benefit from being stored in an airtight container, but not together! Crisp cookies will become limp if stored with soft ones, so make sure to have enough tins and airtight containers for all of your various cookies. Also, make sure to cool cookies completely before placing them in a storage container or the heat might create condensation.

There is a product called Blue Magic, which helps crisp cookies stay that way. It is a small device a little larger than a walnut that has a clear glass bottom and perforated metal top. Inside is a dry chemical that absorbs moisture. You place one of these devices in your cookie jar and it absorbs any moisture so that crisp foods stay crisp. It's called "blue" magic because the chemical changes from blue to pinkish-white as it absorbs moisture. When it has completely turned pinkish-white, you just dry it out in the oven or toaster oven; when it's blue again, it's ready to use once more. It is inexpensive and can be mail-ordered (see Resources).

For soft cookies, there is something called a Brown Sugar Bear, which is a small piece of terra cotta shaped like a teddy bear. Sometimes it is just a disc of terra cotta. You soak it in water, then place it in a container with soft cookies to help retain their texture. You can also place it in a container of brown sugar to help keep it soft (see Resources).

Sending Cookies by Mail

A mailed gift-package of cookies is always well received, but you want to make sure they arrive in as good condition as when they were cooling in your kitchen.

First, choose your cookies wisely. Some bar cookies make good choices for mailing as do soft cookies without any soft frosting or icing. Firm, crisp cookies, such as shortbread, are a good choice too. Steer clear of lacy or delicate cookies, which break easily. In individual recipes, I have pointed out with a special icon ⊠ which cookies I think survive the mailing process the best.

Begin by packing each kind of cookie in its own small tin or airtight plastic container. I go to the dollar store and load up. Make sure the shapes of the containers are large enough to allow cookies to lay flat on the bottom. Make a single layer of cookies, top with a piece of parchment, cut to fit, and proceed to add layers of cookies, without overlapping cookies on any given layer. When they overlap, they are more prone to breakage. The last layer should be near the top of the container. Crumble plastic wrap and lay it over the top layer of cookies, then press the top of the container down onto the cushioned layer of plastic wrap. Gently shake the container; the cookies

should not have any wiggle room. If there is still too much air space and the cookies are moving around, add more plastic wrap.

Once each of your different kinds of cookies is wrapped in its own container, place the various containers in a large sturdy box that has been partially filled with Styrofoam "peanuts" packing material, then top off with more peanuts before sealing the box. You want to fill up the outer box with peanuts so that the individual containers are as snug as possible and don't swim around in the box. Alternatively, tape all of the cookie containers together and wrap completely with bubble-wrap so that the entire package fits snugly inside your outer box. You can also use crumbled newspaper in lieu of peanuts.

Chewy vs. Crispy vs. Soft vs. Cakey Chocolate Chip Cookies—Have It Your Way

When it comes to chocolate chip cookies, people definitely have strong opinions. If you lean towards being a crispy-type cookie person, then a chewy cookie is just not going to satisfy.

I tend to like chewy, so the recipes in this book that are based on classic chocolate chip cookie dough are geared towards that goal. I define a chewy chocolate chip cookie as one cooked a little more around the edges, where a firm, sugary, buttery rim will result, but with a chewy center. The good news is that if you like crispy, all you have to do is bake the very same cookies a minute or two longer. That's it! No change has to be made to the formulation of the dough.

Another way to create a chewy cookie is to use vegetable shortening instead of butter. You could replace the entire amount, use half and half, or whatever proportion you like. The cookies will be chewy (if not overbaked) and will have a very long lifespan, due to the addition of shortening. They will also be a bit paler than those made with all butter. Some folks add a tablespoon or two of corn syrup to add color and chew and this is a technique to consider. I think there is a compromise to the flavor, but to each his own! Also, if you do want to use shortening, you have a choice of regular or butter-flavored, but know that the latter has flavorings added and doesn't really taste like butter. Cookies made with shortening will also

have the added bonus of not spreading flat. Cookies with shortening retain their shape quite nicely.

If you like your cookies soft throughout, with a slightly doughy quality, then there is another approach to take. Simply preheat your oven to 325°F, as opposed to the traditional 375°F, and bake the cookies until very light golden brown all over. Cool them on the pans for a few minutes to firm up. The entire cookie will remain soft.

If you like a cakier style, then you could try adding a bit more flour. Try the recipe as it is written first, then make an assessment. I suggest beginning with 2 tablespoons more flour first, then increasing by 2-tablespoon increments until you get the desired effect. You will probably have to increase the baking time slightly as well.

How to Control Chocolate Chip Cookies that Spread Flat

Some cookies spread thin during baking. It is a trait loved by some and condemned by others. Regardless of what camp you are in, it pays to know how to control it.

- Chilling the dough before baking reduces spread. (Some recipes don't

How to Bake Perfect Cookies

- Read every recipe through before starting
- Use the ingredients called for (for instance, do not substitute extra-large eggs for large)
- Take time to measure accurately with the proper tools
- Use the time cues and visual cues given in the recipe when mixing and baking for best results
- Do not overbake—I believe the number-one problem with baking cookies is overbaking
- Cool cookies properly
- Store cookies according to individual instructions
- Relax and enjoy the baking process!

18

need chilling to keep their shape, but try chilling the dough if you want more shape to your cookies.)

- I like to use butter for its exceptional flavor. Unfortunately, it encourages spreading. If you want, you can try substituting vegetable shortening or butter-flavored shortening for part or all of the butter and see if you like the results.
- Bleached flours sometimes reduce spread. Check your flour. If you are using unbleached flour, that might be encouraging spread.
- Parchment paper reduces spread; ungreased cookie sheets encourage spread, as the heat is more direct.
- Use a scoop to form drop cookies; it helps compact the dough and reduce spread.
- Placing cookie dough on a warm cookie sheet encourages spread.
- Try baking your cookies on another rack in the oven; some ovens vary greatly and, depending on where the heat source is, one rack might encourage spread while another retards it.

The Percentage of Chocolate vs. Dough Conundrum

Ah, yes, the chocolate to dough ratio question…are you a dough lover or a chocolate morsel addict? My take on it is that the cookie dough makes the morsels taste that much better and vice versa. If I wanted plain chocolate, I would just eat it out of hand. So, in these recipes, for the most part (unless noted otherwise), the cookies feature a nice amount of dough and a good quantity of morsels. I have attempted to strike a balance.

If you want more morsels in your cookies, go right ahead and add them. As always, I suggest that you prepare the cookies as stated in the recipe at least once. That way you will have a baseline for future tinkering. In many cases, you can add up to double the amount of chips. The addition of more chocolate will probably affect the way they bake, however, so keep an eye on the baking time and, of course, your yield will increase.

How to Make Your Chocolate Chip Cookies Look Picture-Perfect

I am sure you have had the experience of buying a bag of cookies based on how yummy and chock-full of chips the cookie looks on the bag. Then, when you pull out the first cookie, what a disappointment! Sure there are chips, but they are far and few between and hard to find amongst all the dough.

There are rare creatures out there called food stylists and their job is to make food look as delectable as possible. That's why the hamburger at the fast-food joint looks nothing like the one in the ad! Anyway, we can use stylist's tips

Do You Love Raw Cookie Dough?

A man who knew I was working on this book volunteered that whenever a chocolate chip recipe said it would make 36 cookies, he would end up with about 28. Then he quickly admitted that it was because he ate a lot of the dough raw! This did not surprise me in the least. I am not even a closeted raw dough eater—I announce the fact loud and clear. I can't resist. I simply love the buttery, sugary mixture.

My point of raising this issue is safety. The dough contains raw eggs. Raw eggs should not be eaten by the very young, very old, or those with a compromised immune system. If you simply cannot resist the temptation and want to be perfectly safe, then use pasteurized eggs. Many supermarkets carry them now.

And if I come into your kitchen and catch you finger-scraping the bowl, I won't tell—as long as you share!

and tricks to make our own chocolate chip cookies have that visual "wow" factor. And it is very easy.

Just reserve some of the chocolate morsels or chips (or chunks or nuts, etc.) called for in the recipe and set them aside. I stated setting aside about 25 percent. So, for every cup of morsels called for in the recipe, set aside ¼ cup and stir the remaining ¾ cup into the dough as directed. After you have portioned the dough onto the cookie sheets, press the reserved morsels (or chunks or whatever) onto the tops of the cookies. This way when they bake, these "extra" morsels will remain on top and give your cookie a very professional, luscious, bursting-with-chips look. It's not cheating! It is a way to make your cookies look as great as they taste.

How to Have Warm-from-the-Oven Cookies Anytime

Few things are as irresistible as meltingly warm, ooey, gooey chocolate chip cook-ies. Well, I've got good news! There are two techniques that can ensure that warm cookies are just a few minutes away.

For cookies that are based on classic chocolate chip cookie dough, or other freezable dough, and are drop cookies, follow this procedure. Chill the dough, then portion out scoops or balls of dough with an ice cream scoop or roll it into balls with your hands. Place the cold balls in a zipper-lock plastic freezer bag and pop it into the freezer. Whenever the yen hits, just bake off a few cookies as you need them. Place the frozen balls on parchment paper–lined cookie sheets to defrost a bit while the oven preheats, then bake them as directed in the particular recipe, though the bake time might be a bit longer because the dough will still be very cold.

Another easy technique is to warm already baked cookies in a preheated 300°F oven just until warmed through. The chocolate will soften and the cookies will have a just-baked quality.

The
Field Guide

Amaretto Almond White Chocolate Squares

♦ TYPE *Bar cookie*

♦ DESCRIPTION *This chewy bar is packed with white chocolate morsels and toasted almonds. Amaretto liqueur enhances the dough before and after baking for a decidedly adult taste and added moistness.*

♦ FIELD NOTES *Amaretto is an almond-flavored liqueur that harmonizes wonderfully with white chocolate.*

♦ LIFESPAN *1 week at room temperature in airtight container*

Yield: *16 bars*

◢ INGREDIENTS

1 cup all-purpose flour
Heaping ½ teaspoon baking powder
⅛ teaspoon salt
½ cup (1 stick) unsalted butter, melted
½ cup granulated sugar
½ cup firmly packed light brown sugar

1 teaspoon vanilla extract
3 tablespoons amaretto liqueur
1 large egg
⅔ cup white chocolate morsels
⅔ cup sliced almonds, toasted (see page 16)

◢ DIRECTIONS

1. Preheat oven to 350°F. Coat an 8-inch square baking pan with nonstick cooking spray.

2. Whisk flour, baking powder, and salt together in a small bowl.

3. In a large bowl, whisk together melted butter, granulated sugar, and brown sugar. Whisk in vanilla, 1 tablespoon of the amaretto, and the egg, blending well. Stir in flour mixture, mixing just until blended. Make sure mixture is cool, then stir in chocolate morsels and half the nuts. Spread evenly into prepared pan. Sprinkle remaining nuts evenly on top of batter.

4. Bake until light golden brown, slightly puffed, and edges have begun to pull away from sides of pan, about 25 minutes. A toothpick inserted in center should come out with some moist crumbs clinging.

5. Brush remaining 2 tablespoons amaretto evenly over squares. Place pan on rack until completely cool. Cut into 16 bars (4 x 4).

Anytime S'Mores

🍫 **TYPE** *Bar cookie*

....

🍫 **DESCRIPTION** *This bar cookie combines the favorite childhood flavors of campfire s'mores—graham crackers, chocolate, and marshmallow. If you have a real sweet tooth, this one's for you.*

....

🍫 **FIELD NOTES** *Classic s'mores (as in "give me some more") are constructed by taking a graham cracker, placing a piece of chocolate on top, and then crowning it with a toasted marshmallow. Part of the fun is finding the perfect, skinny stick to use as a marshmallow-roasting device. Fresh, green sticks won't burn and finding the right length is important too. Then there are the various techniques for the actual campfire marshmallow toasting, which range from gentle, even browning to engulfing the marshmallow in flames. With this recipe, you control the browning under the broiler.*

....

🍫 **RELATED SPECIES** *You can use all milk chocolate morsels, all semisweet chocolate morsels, or even leave out the morsels on top; it's your choice.*

....

🍫 **LIFESPAN** *1 week at room temperature in airtight container in single layers separated by waxed (or parchment) paper*

Yield: *16 bars*

◢ INGREDIENTS

½ cup (1 stick) unsalted butter, softened
2 cups graham cracker crumbs (from 16 sheets of crackers)
1½ cups milk chocolate morsels

One 14-ounce can sweetened condensed milk
2 cups miniature marshmallows
⅔ cup semisweet chocolate morsels

◢ DIRECTIONS

1. Preheat oven to 350°F.

2. Place butter in 9-inch square baking pan and set in oven while it preheats until butter melts. Remove from oven, add graham cracker crumbs, and stir to combine well. Pat buttered crumbs into an even layer. Sprinkle milk chocolate morsels evenly over crust, then drizzle condensed milk over morsels.

3. Bake until golden brown and bubbly, about 30 minutes. Place pan on rack to cool slightly while you preheat broiler. Adjust rack in oven close to broiler.

4. Sprinkle marshmallows evenly over top and broil until they are lightly browned, about 2 minutes, turning pan front to back at least once to encourage even browning. Remove pan from broiler, place on rack, and sprinkle semisweet morsels over top. Allow to cool at least 15 minutes more before cutting into 16 bars (4 x 4).

Applesauce Oaties with White Chocolate Chips, Raisins, and Walnuts

TYPE *Drop cookie*

DESCRIPTION *Applesauce makes these cookies moist and good keepers. They are not terribly sweet, even though they are packed with chips, two kinds of raisins, and toasted walnuts.*

FIELD NOTES *While I am a big fan of homemade applesauce, you can use purchased unsweetened applesauce for this recipe with no loss of flavor.*

LIFESPAN *1 week at room temperature in airtight container*

Yield: *45 cookies*

◆ INGREDIENTS

2½ cups oats (use old-fashioned, not quick
  or instant)
1½ cups all-purpose flour
1 cup white chocolate morsels
1 cup walnut halves, toasted (see page 16)
  and chopped
½ cup dark raisins
½ cup golden raisins
1½ teaspoons ground cinnamon

1 teaspoon baking soda
¼ teaspoon baking powder
¼ teaspoon salt
1 cup (2 sticks) unsalted butter, melted
1 cup firmly packed dark brown sugar
1 cup unsweetened applesauce
1 teaspoon vanilla extract
1 large egg

◆ DIRECTIONS

1. Whisk oats, flour, chocolate morsels, nuts, both raisins, cinnamon, baking soda, baking powder, and salt together in a large bowl.

2. In another large bowl, whisk together melted butter and brown sugar. Whisk in applesauce and vanilla, then the egg, blending well. Stir in dry mixture, mixing just until blended. Cover with plastic wrap and chill dough at least 2 hours, or overnight.

3. Preheat oven to 325°F. Line 2 cookie sheets with parchment paper.

4. Drop chilled dough by generously rounded tablespoon 2 inches apart on prepared cookie sheets and flatten with floured fingers to about ½-inch thickness. Bake until edges and tops turn light golden brown, about 12 minutes. Place sheets on racks to cool completely.

Apricot Almond White Chocolate Chip Cookies

🍫 **TYPE** *Drop cookie*

🍫 **DESCRIPTION** *This is a classic chocolate chip cookie dough with the addition of almond extract, chopped apricots, sliced almonds, and white chocolate morsels.*

🍫 **FIELD NOTES** *The almond extract enhances not only the almonds but the apricots. As with vanilla extract, make sure to use pure almond extract. You can use blanched or natural (skin on) almonds, but I like the look of the natural ones in this recipe.*

🍫 **RELATED SPECIES** *Tipsy Apricot Almond White Chocolate Chip Cookies: Toss the chopped apricots with 1 or 2 tablespoons apricot brandy for a grown-up touch. Add an additional tablespoon of flour if you do.*

🍫 **LIFESPAN** *1 week at room temperature in airtight container*

Yield: *54 cookies*

● INGREDIENTS

2¼ cups all-purpose flour
1 teaspoon baking soda
1 teaspoon salt
1 cup (2 sticks) unsalted butter, softened
¾ cup granulated sugar
¾ cup firmly packed light brown sugar
1 teaspoon vanilla extract

¼ teaspoon almond extract
2 large eggs
1 cup white chocolate morsels
1 cup sliced almonds, toasted (see page 16)
1 cup chopped dried apricots

● DIRECTIONS

1. Whisk flour, baking soda, and salt together in a medium-size bowl.

2. In a large bowl with an electric mixer on medium-high speed, beat butter until creamy, about 2 minutes. Add granulated sugar and brown sugar gradually, beating until light and fluffy, about 3 minutes, and scraping down bowl once or twice. Beat in extracts, then eggs, one at a time, scraping down bowl. Add about one-third of flour mixture and mix on low speed. Gradually add remaining flour mixture, mixing just until blended. Stir in chocolate morsels, almonds, and apricots. Cover with plastic wrap and chill dough at least 2 hours or overnight.

3. Preheat oven to 375°F. Line 2 cookie sheets with parchment paper.

4. Drop chilled dough by generously rounded tablespoon 2 inches apart on prepared cookie sheets. Bake until edges and tops just begin to turn light golden brown, about 12 minutes. Place sheets on racks to cool cookies completely.

Bittersweet Chocolate Chip Raspberry Truffle Brownies

🍫 **TYPE** *Bar cookie*

🍫 **DESCRIPTION** *Mmmmm, raspberries and chocolate! These feature a light cocoa brownie studded with fresh raspberries and bittersweet chocolate bits. A deep, velvety truffle-like ganache crowns each brownie. They are also enhanced by framboise, a raspberry eau de vie, making these a very adult brownie; they are actually kind of light and not too rich. While the eau de vie is not appealing to kids, they love to help press the raspberries into the batter.*

🍫 **FIELD NOTES** *The late Michael McLaughlin was a prolific cookbook author and fellow* Bon Appétit *magazine contributor. Early in my food writing career he took the time to guide me and answer questions whenever I called. He probably didn't realize that I considered him a mentor. These brownies are based upon a recipe of his. Michael, these are for you.*

🍫 **LIFESPAN** *2 days at room temperature in airtight container if unfrosted; eat same day if frosted*

Yield: *32 bars*

🍫 INGREDIENTS

Brownies:

1¼ cups all-purpose flour
½ cup Dutch-processed unsweetened
  cocoa powder
¼ teaspoon salt
1 cup (2 sticks) unsalted butter, softened
1¼ cups granulated sugar
½ cup firmly packed light brown sugar
1 tablespoon framboise
1 teaspoon vanilla extract

4 large eggs
⅓ cup finely chopped bittersweet
  chocolate (about 1½ ounces)
1½ cups fresh raspberries

Frosting:

7 ounces bittersweet chocolate, finely
  chopped
½ cup heavy cream
1 teaspoon framboise

🍫 DIRECTIONS

1. Preheat oven to 350°F. Coat a 9 x 13-inch baking pan with nonstick cooking spray.

2. Sift flour, cocoa, and salt together in a small bowl.

3. In a large bowl with an electric mixer on medium-high speed, beat butter until creamy, about 2 minutes. Add granulated sugar and brown sugar gradually, beating until light and fluffy, about 3 minutes, and scraping down bowl once or twice. Beat in framboise and vanilla, then eggs, one at a time, scraping down bowl. Add about one-third of flour mixture and mix on low speed. Gradually add remaining flour mixture, mixing just until blended. Batter will be thick. Stir in chocolate and spread evenly in prepared pan. Scatter raspberries evenly over top and gently press into batter until submerged.

4. Bake until slightly puffed and edges have begun to pull away from sides of pan, about 30 minutes. A toothpick inserted in center should come out with some moist crumbs clinging. Place pan on rack until completely cool.

5. To make frosting, place chopped chocolate in a heatproof bowl. Bring cream to a boil in a saucepan over medium heat. Immediately pour over chocolate; allow to sit for a few minutes for heat of cream to melt chocolate, then stir gently until ganache is smooth. Stir in framboise. Allow to cool at room temperature until thick enough to spread, about the consistency of soft mayonnaise. Spread evenly over cooled brownies using a small offset spatula. Cut into 32 bars (8 x 4).

Bittersweet Chocolate Nib Cookies

🍫 **TYPE** *Drop cookie*

🍫 **DESCRIPTION** *These chocolate chip cookies combine bittersweet chocolate chunks with cacao nibs in a brown sugar chocolate chip cookie dough. The nibs are the actual roasted and shelled cacao beans broken into tiny pieces. They taste like pure chocolate, without added sugar.*

🍫 **FIELD NOTES** *At first, cacao nibs might seem odd. If you taste them plain, they don't taste like anything else you have ever encountered. But if you are a chocolate lover, these will grow on you—fast!—and you will find ways to incorporate them into your own recipes. I use Scharffen Berger Cacao Nibs, which are available nationwide. Whole Foods stores carry them, as does Sweet Celebrations (see Resources).*

🍫 **LIFESPAN** *1 week at room temperature in airtight container*

Yield: *50 cookies*

● INGREDIENTS

2¼ cups all-purpose flour
1 teaspoon baking soda
1 teaspoon salt
1 cup (2 sticks) unsalted butter, softened
¾ cup granulated sugar
¾ cup firmly packed light brown sugar

1 teaspoon vanilla extract
2 large eggs
2 cups bittersweet chocolate chunks
  (¼-inch), about 10 ounces
½ cup cacao nibs

● DIRECTIONS

1. Whisk flour, baking soda, and salt together in a medium-size bowl.

2. In a large bowl with an electric mixer on medium-high speed, beat butter until creamy, about 2 minutes. Add granulated sugar and brown sugar gradually, beating until light and fluffy, about 3 minutes, and scraping down bowl once or twice. Beat in vanilla, then eggs, one at a time, scraping down bowl. Add about one-third of flour mixture and mix on low speed. Gradually add remaining flour mixture, mixing just until blended. Stir in chocolate chunks and nibs. Cover with plastic wrap and chill dough at least 2 hours or overnight.

3. Preheat oven to 375°F. Line 2 cookie sheets with parchment paper.

4. Drop chilled dough by generously rounded tablespoon 2 inches apart on prepared cookie sheets. Bake until edges and tops just begin to turn light golden brown, about 12 minutes. Slide parchment onto racks to cool cookies completely.

Black and White Rice Crispy Bars

🍫 **TYPE** *Bar cookie*

🍫 **DESCRIPTION** *These bars are very easy to make and combine crisp puffed rice cereal, melted marshmallows, and both white and semisweet chocolate morsels. You get two treats in one; the bottom layer is studded with semisweet chocolate morsels, while the top half is flavored and colored with cocoa and studded with white chocolate morsels. I suggest piling them on a platter with half facing light side up, the other half featuring the dark cocoa side.*

🍫 **FIELD NOTES** *You can use 24 ounces of any kind of marshmallow but the miniature ones melt evenly and easily. Make sure to allow the marshmallow-cereal mixture to cool slightly before folding in the morsels or they will melt. The bars will still taste great; they just won't be as pretty or dramatic. This folding process is sticky and difficult, by the way. Just keep at it.*

🍫 **LIFESPAN** *1 week at room temperature in airtight container*

Yield: *24 bars*

🍫 INGREDIENTS

Light layer:
- 3 tablespoons unsalted butter
- 12 ounces miniature marshmallows
- 6 cups puffed rice cereal (such as Rice Krispies)
- ¾ cup semisweet chocolate morsels

Dark layer:
- 3 tablespoons unsalted butter
- 2 tablespoons Dutch-processed unsweetened cocoa powder
- 12 ounces miniature marshmallows
- 6 cups puffed rice cereal (such as Rice Krispies)
- ¾ cup white chocolate morsels

🍫 DIRECTIONS

1. Coat a 9 x 13-inch baking pan with nonstick cooking spray.

2. For light layer, melt butter in a large saucepan over medium heat. Add marshmallows and stir to coat. Melt marshmallows, stirring frequently.

3. Place cereal in a large bowl. Remove marshmallow mixture from heat and scrape over cereal, stirring well to coat. Mixture will be sticky. Just keep folding and stirring to coat cereal evenly and to cool mixture. Fold in semisweet chocolate morsels and immediately spread into prepared pan. Use your hands to evenly press mixture into pan, including corners.

4. For dark layer, melt butter in clean large saucepan over medium heat. Whisk in cocoa, then marshmallows and stir to coat. Melt marshmallows, stirring frequently.

5. Place cereal in clean large bowl. Remove marshmallow mixture from heat and scrape over cereal, stirring well to coat and to cool mixture. Fold in white chocolate morsels and immediately spread into prepared pan over first layer. Use your hands to press into an even layer.

6. Allow mixture to cool, then cut into 24 bars (6 x 4).

Black-Bottom, Creamy, Chippy Cookie Cupcakes

🍫 **TYPE** *Molded cookie*

🍫 **DESCRIPTION** *These are miniature cupcakes, but, like a cookie, they are tiny and easy to eat. They combine a chocolate cake batter studded with mini chocolate morsels and a cheesecake filling.*

🍫 **FIELD NOTES** *These will taste great no matter how sloppily you add the cheesecake filling, but if you are very careful, and center a dollop of filling in the middle of the cake batter, they will bake with a striking bull's-eye pattern that adds to their charm. Also, note that I had the best success with dark nonstick muffin tins for this recipe. They seemed to bake these cupcakes most evenly.*

🍫 **RELATED SPECIES** Great Big Black-Bottom, Creamy, Chippy Cookie Cupcakes: *While these are adorable in a mini version, you can make them in standard-size muffin cups. Use a generous double amount of cake batter and filling and bake them about 18 minutes, using the same visual cues to test for doneness.*

🍫 **LIFESPAN** *4 days at room temperature in airtight container in single layers separated by waxed (or parchment) paper*

☺

Yield: *50 miniature cupcakes*

🍫 **INGREDIENTS**

Batter:
1½ cups all-purpose flour
¼ cup Dutch-processed unsweetened
  cocoa powder
1 teaspoon baking soda
½ teaspoon salt
1 cup granulated sugar
½ cup miniature semisweet chocolate
  morsels
1 cup warm water

⅓ cup light, flavorless vegetable oil
1 tablespoon distilled white or cider
  vinegar
1 tablespoon vanilla extract

Filling:
One 8-ounce package cream cheese,
  softened
½ cup granulated sugar
¼ teaspoon vanilla extract
1 large egg

🍫 **DIRECTIONS**

1. Preheat oven to 350°F. Coat tops of four 12-cup mini-muffin tins with non-stick cooking spray; line them with mini paper liners.

2. Sift flour, cocoa, baking soda, salt, and sugar together in a large bowl; stir in miniature chocolate morsels.

3. Make a well in middle of dry mixture and, one by one, add the water, oil, vinegar, and vanilla. Whisk until smooth.

4. In a medium-size bowl with an electric mixer on medium-high speed, beat cream cheese until creamy, about 2 minutes. Add sugar and vanilla, beating until light and fluffy, about 3 minutes, and scraping down bowl once or twice. Beat in egg.

5. Place about 1 tablespoon of chocolate batter in each mini paper liner. It should come up just above halfway. Then spoon a teaspoon-size dollop of cheesecake filling in the very center of each cupcake. The neater you do this and the rounder the shape of the cheesecake batter (you can use a mini

ice cream scoop or melon baller), the more striking the results. You want it to look like a bull's-eye.

6. Bake until a toothpick comes out clean when inserted in the chocolate batter, about 12 minutes. Place tins on racks for 5 minutes, then unmold cupcakes and place directly on racks to cool completely. To help remove from tins, insert the tip of a butter knife between the cupcake and the tin and gently apply inward and upward pressure to release it.

Good Cookie Tip

The reason you spray the tops of the muffin tins with nonstick spray is because some of the batter might puff up and come in contact with that surface. The spraying ensures easy unmolding. In fact, I always spray the tops of the tins whenever I make muffins or cupcakes of any sort.

37

Black Forest Chocolate Chip Cookies

🍫 **TYPE** *Drop cookie*

🍫 **DESCRIPTION** *The term "black forest" refers to the chocolate and cherries in the batter, a flavor combination taken from the classic German Black Forest cake. Kirsch is an eau de vie made from ripe cherries that are crushed, pressed, fermented, and distilled. It is used here to plump the dried cherries, making these very adult cookies.*

🍫 **FIELD NOTES** *Dried cherries are fairly easy to find at specialty stores and through mail order. You can buy sweet dried cherries, but I prefer the tart variety. Some of them have sugar added, but they are still sour-ish, which I think adds a nice dimension and counterpoint to the bittersweet chocolate.*

🍫 **RELATED SPECIES** *Check out* Chocolate Chip Cherry Mandelbrot *on page 58.*

🍫 **LIFESPAN** *1 week at room temperature in airtight container*

Yield: *55 cookies*

🍫 INGREDIENTS

1⅓ cups dried tart cherries, chopped
½ cup kirsch
2⅓ cups plus 1 tablespoon all-purpose flour
1 teaspoon baking soda
1 teaspoon salt
1 cup (2 sticks) unsalted butter, softened

¾ cup granulated sugar
¾ cup firmly packed light brown sugar
1 teaspoon vanilla extract
¼ teaspoon almond extract
2 large eggs
3 cups bittersweet chocolate chunks (⅓-inch), about 15 ounces

🍫 DIRECTIONS

1. Combine chopped cherries and kirsch in a microwaveable bowl and heat on high power for 1 minute. Allow to sit for 15 minutes for kirsch to permeate the cherries. Alternatively, combine in a small saucepan, bring to a boil over medium heat, then remove from heat to soak while you prepare the dough. This plumps and flavors the cherries.

2. Whisk flour, baking soda, and salt together in a medium-size bowl.

3. In a large bowl with an electric mixer on medium-high speed, beat butter until creamy, about 2 minutes. Add granulated sugar and brown sugar gradually, beating until light and fluffy, about 3 minutes, and scraping down bowl once or twice. Beat in extracts, then eggs, one at a time, scraping down bowl. Add about one-third of flour mixture and mix on low speed. Gradually add remaining flour mixture, mixing just until blended. Stir in chocolate chunks and cooled,

plumped cherries, including up to 1 tablespoon of any remaining liquid; discard the rest. Cover with plastic wrap and chill dough 2 hours or overnight.

4. Preheat oven to 375°F. Line 2 cookie sheets with parchment paper.

5. Drop chilled dough by generously rounded tablespoon 2 inches apart on prepared cookie sheets. Bake until edges and tops just begin to turn light golden brown, about 12 minutes. These will be thin and somewhat delicate. Place sheets on racks to cool cookies completely.

Good Cookie Tip

Chopping dried fruit can sometimes be a sticky problem. You can chop the cherries in a food processor or try coating the blade of a heavy chef's knife with nonstick cooking spray and chopping them by hand.

Blondies

🍫 **TYPE** *Bar cookie*

🍫 **DESCRIPTION** *These have chocolate chips and walnuts added to a chewy dough rich in brown sugar and butter.*

🍫 **FIELD NOTES** *Including blondies in the book was an obvious choice. They are probably the #1 non-chocolate brownie type of bar cookie that features chocolate chips.*

🍫 **RELATED SPECIES** *Blondies can be varied easily and endlessly. Try milk chocolate chips and pecans, or one or the other. Or, in addition to chocolate morsels, try peanut butter chips or butterscotch chips.*

🍫 **LIFESPAN** *1 week at room temperature in airtight container*

Yield: *16 bars*

INGREDIENTS

1 cup all-purpose flour
Heaping ½ teaspoon baking powder
⅛ teaspoon salt
½ cup (1 stick) unsalted butter, melted
1 cup firmly packed light brown sugar

1 teaspoon vanilla extract
1 large egg
⅔ cup semisweet chocolate morsels
⅔ cup walnut halves, toasted (see
   page 16) and chopped

DIRECTIONS

1. Preheat oven to 350°F. Coat an 8-inch square baking pan with nonstick cooking spray.

2. Whisk flour, baking powder, and salt together in a small bowl.

3. In a large bowl, whisk together melted butter and brown sugar. Whisk in vanilla, then the egg, blending well. Stir in flour mixture, mixing just until blended. Make sure mixture is cool, then stir in chocolate morsels and nuts. Spread evenly in prepared pan.

4. Bake until light golden brown, slightly puffed, and edges have begun to pull away from sides of pan, about 25 minutes. A toothpick inserted in center should come out with some moist crumbs clinging. Place pan on rack to cool completely. Cut into 16 bars (4 x 4).

Browned-Butter Bourbon Pecan Cookies with Milk Chocolate Chips

🍫 **TYPE** *Drop cookie*

🍫 **DESCRIPTION** *This is a not-too-sweet crumbly cookie with ground pecans in the batter as well as chopped pecans that have been sautéed in browned butter—and a splash of bourbon thrown in for good measure.*

🍫 **FIELD NOTES** *I have tried to make this cookie many ways, but they come out the best when one part is made in the food processor and the other in the mixer. Sorry for the extra work but you won't mind so much once you taste them.*

🍫 **LIFESPAN** *1 week at room temperature in airtight container*

Yield: *50 cookies*

● INGREDIENTS

1 tablespoon plus 1 teaspoon unsalted butter
1¾ cups pecan halves
1½ cups all-purpose flour
½ teaspoon salt
1 cup (2 sticks) unsalted butter, softened

¾ cup firmly packed light brown sugar
2 teaspoons bourbon
1 teaspoon vanilla extract
1 large egg
½ cup milk chocolate morsels

● DIRECTIONS

1. Melt butter in medium-size skillet over medium heat until browned. Add 1¼ cups of the pecan halves and stir to coat. Cook for a few minutes, stirring frequently, until they begin to brown. Remove from heat and allow to cool. Remove 50 pecan halves and set aside. Chop the rest.

2. Place the remaining ½ cup unsautéed pecan halves, the flour, and salt in a food processor and pulse to chop, then process until nuts are finely ground.

3. In a large bowl with an electric mixer on medium-high speed, beat butter until creamy, about 2 minutes. Add brown sugar gradually, beating until light and fluffy, about 3 minutes, and scraping down bowl once or twice. Beat in bourbon and vanilla, then egg. Add about one-third of flour mixture and mix on low speed. Gradually add remaining flour mixture, mixing just until blended. Stir in chocolate morsels and chopped pecans. Cover with plastic wrap and chill dough 2 hours or overnight.

4. Preheat oven to 350°F. Line 2 cookie sheets with parchment paper.

5. Drop chilled dough by generously rounded tablespoon 2 inches apart on prepared cookie sheets. Flatten slightly with your floured palm as you also press a pecan half, rounded side up, in the center of each cookie. Cookies should be about ½ inch thick. Bake until edges and tops just begin to turn light golden brown, about 13 minutes. Let sheets cool on racks for 5 minutes, then slide parchment onto racks to let cookies cool completely.

Buttermilk Chocolate Chip Brownies with Coconut Pecan Frosting

🍫 **TYPE** *Bar cookie*

🍫 **DESCRIPTION** *This recipe makes a big batch of soft, cocoa-flavored buttermilk brownies covered with miniature chocolate morsels. The frosting is sweet, sticky, and full of coconut and pecans. These are very moist and keep very well.*

🍫 **FIELD NOTES** *These brownies are based on the classic German chocolate cake, which features a chocolate cake and a unique coconut-pecan frosting that is cooked on top of the stove.*

🍫 **LIFESPAN** *1 week at room temperature in an airtight container in single layers separated by waxed (or parchment) paper*

Yield: *32 bars*

🍫 INGREDIENTS

Brownies:
- 2 cups all-purpose flour
- 1 cup granulated sugar
- 1 cup firmly packed light brown sugar
- 1 teaspoon baking soda
- 1 cup (2 sticks) unsalted butter, softened
- ½ cup buttermilk (preferably lowfat)
- 1 cup water
- ⅓ cup Dutch-processed unsweetened cocoa powder
- 1 teaspoon vanilla extract
- 1 teaspoon almond extract
- 2 large eggs
- ½ cup miniature semisweet chocolate morsels

Frosting:
- 1 cup evaporated milk
- 1 cup granulated sugar
- 3 large egg yolks
- ½ cup (1 stick) unsalted butter, softened
- 1 teaspoon vanilla extract
- 1½ cups sweetened flaked coconut
- 1 cup pecan halves, toasted (see page 16) and chopped

🍫 DIRECTIONS

1. Preheat oven to 350°F. Coat a 9 x 13-inch baking pan with nonstick cooking spray.

2. Whisk flour, both sugars, and baking soda together in a large bowl. Make a well in center and set aside.

3. Melt butter in a medium-size saucepan over medium heat. Remove from heat, then whisk in buttermilk, water, and cocoa until smooth. Whisk in extracts, then eggs, one at a time. Slowly pour wet ingredients into well in dry mixture and whisk constantly until smooth. Pour into prepared pan.

4. Bake until edges are puffed and top is dry, about 20 minutes. Sprinkle top evenly with morsels. Continue to bake until a toothpick inserted in center comes out with just a few moist crumbs, about 15 minutes more. Place pan on rack to cool completely.

5. To make frosting, whisk together evaporated milk and granulated sugar in large saucepan. Whisk in egg yolks and softened butter. Gently cook over medium heat until mixture reaches a simmer, then reduce heat to low and cook, whisking frequently, until it slightly darkens and thickens, about 10 minutes. Remove from heat and stir in vanilla, coconut, and pecans. Let cool, stirring occasionally to release heat, until just warm to the touch and thick.

6. Spread frosting evenly over brownies. Cut into 32 bars (8 x 4).

Cappuccino Chocolate Chip Biscotti Dunkers

🍫 **TYPE** *Shaped cookie*

. . . .

🍫 **DESCRIPTION** *These biscotti taste like a cappuccino in a cookie, where the flavors of espresso, cinnamon, and a dusting of cocoa converge in every bite.*

. . . .

🍫 **FIELD NOTES** *These have no added butter so they are low fat and very crispy crunchy. Take the time to slice them thinly to make a very elegant presentation.*

. . . .

🍫 **LIFESPAN** *1 month at room temperature in airtight container*

Yield: *36 biscotti*

🍫 INGREDIENTS

Biscotti:
2 cups all-purpose flour
⅔ cup granulated sugar
1 teaspoon ground cinnamon
½ teaspoon baking powder
½ teaspoon baking soda
3 large eggs
1 tablespoon freshly ground espresso beans
1 teaspoon vanilla extract
1 cup milk chocolate morsels

Topping:
¼ cup granulated sugar
½ teaspoon ground cinnamon
½ teaspoon Dutch-processed unsweetened cocoa powder

🍫 DIRECTIONS

1. Whisk flour, sugar, cinnamon, baking powder, and baking soda together in a large bowl. Using an electric mixer, beat eggs into flour mixture, one at a time, on low speed until well mixed, scraping down bowl once or twice. Beat in espresso and vanilla. Mixture will be thick. Beat in chocolate morsels. Cover with plastic wrap and chill dough until firm enough to roll, at least 30 minutes or overnight.

2. Preheat oven to 350°F. Line 2 cookie sheets with parchment paper. Stir together the topping ingredients in a small bowl; set aside.

3. Roll chilled dough on lightly floured work surface into logs about 1¼ inches wide and 12 inches long. Place 2 logs on one prepared cookie sheet, the third log on the other. Sprinkle logs evenly with topping.

4. Bake until dry to touch and light golden brown around edges and over top, about 25 minutes. Remove from oven and let cool 2 minutes by placing pans on racks.

5. Gently remove each log from pan and place on a cutting board. Diagonally slice biscotti very thinly, about ¼ inch thick, making biscotti about 6 inches long. Place slices back on cookie sheets cut side down and about ¼ inch apart. Bake 6 minutes, flip them, and bake until slices are dry, about 6 minutes more. Slide parchment onto racks to cool cookies completely.

Caramel Chocolate Turtle Cookies

TYPE *Drop cookie*

DESCRIPTION *These combine chocolate chip cookies with whole pecans, a layer of caramel, and a bit of chocolate on top.*

FIELD NOTES *These look like little turtles, if you use your imagination! They are a takeoff on caramel-chocolate-pecan turtle candies, but these incorporate chocolate chip cookie dough into the mix. Kids love to eat and to help make these.*

LIFESPAN *4 days at room temperature in airtight container in single layers separated by waxed (or parchment) paper*

**Good
Cookie Tip**

Make sure your pecan
halves are not broken.
"Whole" pecan halves will
make the best "feet"
and "heads."

Yield: *45 turtles*

⬤ INGREDIENTS

45 Kraft caramels
2½ cups all-purpose flour
1 teaspoon baking soda
1 teaspoon salt
1 cup (2 sticks) unsalted butter, softened
¾ cup granulated sugar
¾ cup firmly packed light brown sugar
1 teaspoon vanilla extract

2 large eggs
2 cups miniature semisweet chocolate
  morsels
3⅔ cups pecan halves (you need 225
  pecan halves, 5 per turtle)
12 ounces semisweet chocolate, finely
  chopped
2 tablespoons vegetable shortening

⬤ DIRECTIONS

1. Unwrap each caramel (they are about
1-inch square and come individually
wrapped) and press flat into a round
shape to about 2 inches across using
your fingers. You want a 2-inch flat
circle about ¼ inch thick; set aside.

2. Whisk flour, baking soda, and salt
together in a medium-size bowl.

3. In a large bowl with an electric mixer
on medium-high speed, beat butter
until creamy, about 2 minutes. Add
granulated sugar and brown sugar
gradually, beating until light and fluffy,
about 3 minutes, and scraping down
bowl once or twice. Beat in vanilla,
then eggs, one at a time, scraping down
bowl. Add about one-third of flour
mixture and mix on low speed.
Gradually add remaining flour mixture,
mixing just until blended. Stir in chocolate morsels. Cover with plastic wrap
and chill at least 2 hours or overnight.

4. Preheat oven to 375°F. Line 2 cookie
sheets with parchment paper.

5. Drop chilled dough by generously
rounded tablespoon 3 inches apart on
prepared cookie sheets. Press 5 pecan
halves into each cookie mound so that
about one quarter of each nut is
embedded in the cookie. You want to

situate them so that they look like the
head and four feet of a turtle; the
rounded side of the pecans should face
up and the bottoms should be flat on
sheet (see photograph). Bake until
edges and tops of cookies have just
begun to turn light golden brown,
about 10 minutes.

6. Center a caramel circle on top of each
cookie and return to oven until cookie
is golden brown and caramel has
softened, but not melted, and is now
part of the cookie (it should be
attached and almost melted onto it),
about 4 minutes. Place sheets on racks
to cool cookies completely.

7. Melt chocolate and shortening
together in a medium-size saucepan
over low heat or in a bowl in a
microwave and stir until smooth.
Pour into a small zipper-lock plastic
bag and seal bag; this is a lot of
chocolate, so you will probably need
to use several bags. Snip a tiny opening
in one corner and decorate the tops
of the turtles by squeezing out chocolate. You can make spirals, crosshatch
patterns, zigzags, etc. You can even
write names of lucky would-be recipi-
ents. Place sheets in refrigerator to firm
up chocolate before storing.

Caramel Surprise
Chocolate Chip Cups

🍫 **TYPE** *Molded cookie*

🍫 **DESCRIPTION** *Chocolate chip cookie dough is baked in a mini-muffin tin, then a chocolate-covered caramel is tucked inside for a tasty, chewy surprise.*

🍫 **FIELD NOTES** *These were inspired by my son Freeman's love of Rolo candies. They come in a roll, all stacked together. Each Rolo is a chocolate-covered caramel candy shaped like a little cupcake and they fit perfectly into the cookie dough, which is partially prebaked in the mini-muffin tins.*

🍫 **LIFESPAN** *4 days at room temperature in airtight container in single layers separated by waxed (or parchment) paper*

Yield: *60 mini cups*

◗ INGREDIENTS

2½ cups all-purpose flour
1 teaspoon baking soda
1 teaspoon salt
1 cup (2 sticks) unsalted butter, softened
¾ cup granulated sugar
¾ cup firmly packed light brown sugar

1 teaspoon vanilla extract
2 large eggs
2 cups miniature semisweet chocolate morsels
60 Rolo candies (you'll need 8 rolls)

◗ DIRECTIONS

1. Preheat oven to 350°F. Coat tops of five 12-cup mini-muffin tins with non-stick cooking spray; line with mini paper liners.

2. Whisk flour, baking soda, and salt together in a medium-size bowl.

3. In a large bowl with an electric mixer on medium-high speed, beat butter until creamy, about 2 minutes. Add granulated sugar and brown sugar gradually, beating until light and fluffy, about 3 minutes, and scraping down bowl once or twice. Beat in vanilla, then eggs, one at a time, scraping down bowl. Add about one-third of flour mixture and mix on low speed.

Gradually add remaining flour mixture, mixing just until blended. Stir in chocolate morsels. Fill each muffin well with about 1 tablespoon of dough.

4. Bake until cups begin to turn light golden brown, about 8 minutes. The insides will still be soft. Press one Rolo candy, narrow side down, into the cup. Leave top of Rolo showing; it should be flush with top of batter. Bake until batter is an even golden brown, about 3 more minutes. Place tins on racks to cool completely before unmolding. To help remove from tins, insert the tip of a butter knife between the cupcake and the tin and gently apply inward and upward pressure to release it.

Chewy Brownie Chip Drops

🍫 **TYPE** *Drop cookie*

🍫 **DESCRIPTION** *These are just like a brownie—soft and chocolatey—but in a handy round cookie shape with chocolate chips and walnuts inside each drop.*

🍫 **FIELD NOTES** *Brownies, which are typically a type of bar cookie, are wonderful as they are, but here they are made as a drop cookie without losing any of their desired qualities.*

🍫 **RELATED SPECIES** *You can easily use milk or white chocolate morsels instead of the semisweet and pecans instead of the walnuts.*

🍫 **LIFESPAN** *4 days at room temperature in airtight container in single layers separated by waxed (or parchment) paper*

Yield: *48 cookies*

🍫 INGREDIENTS

2¼ cups all-purpose flour
⅔ cup Dutch-processed unsweetened
  cocoa powder
1 teaspoon baking soda
1 teaspoon salt
1½ cups (3 sticks) unsalted butter,
  softened

1 cup granulated sugar
⅔ cup firmly packed light brown sugar
2 teaspoons vanilla extract
2 large eggs
1 cup semisweet chocolate morsels
1 cup walnut halves, toasted (see page 16)
  and chopped

🍫 DIRECTIONS

1. Preheat oven to 350°F. Line 2 cookie sheets with parchment paper.

2. Sift flour, cocoa, baking soda, and salt together in a medium-size bowl.

3. In a large bowl with an electric mixer on medium-high speed, beat butter until creamy, about 2 minutes. Add granulated sugar and brown sugar gradually, beating until light and fluffy, about 3 minutes, and scraping down bowl once or twice. Beat in vanilla, then eggs, one at a time, scraping down bowl. Add about one-third of flour mixture and mix on low speed.

Gradually add remaining flour mixture, mixing just until blended. Stir in chocolate morsels and nuts. Drop by generously rounded tablespoon 2 inches apart on prepared cookie sheets.

4. Bake until firmed up around the edges but still a bit soft in the center, about 10 minutes (you want to keep them chewy). Slide parchment onto racks to cool cookies completely.

**Good
Cookie Tip**

These cookies are so dark
that it's hard to gauge doneness
by color. Follow these textural
clues: they should be firm
around the edges, yet soft
in the center.

Chewy Chocolate Chip Cherry Toffee Brownie Drops

🍫 **TYPE** *Drop cookie*

🍫 **DESCRIPTION** *These dark, chewy, brownie-like cookies are embellished with dried tart cherries and shavings of bittersweet chocolate. Make sure to use a high-quality bittersweet chocolate, such as Scharffen Berger or Valrhona.*

🍫 **FIELD NOTES** *I absolutely love Skor Toffee Bits. Keep some in your pantry and you will come up with delicious uses for them. I have tossed the toffee pieces with the flour to help them retain their shape and crunch, as they have a tendency to melt out when baked.*

🍫 **LIFESPAN** *1 week at room temperature in airtight container in single layers separated by waxed (or parchment) paper*

Yield: *56 cookies*

🍫 INGREDIENTS

2¼ cups plus 1 tablespoon all-purpose flour

⅔ cup Dutch-processed unsweetened cocoa powder

1 teaspoon baking soda

1 teaspoon salt

1 cup toffee pieces, such as Skor

1½ cups (3 sticks) unsalted butter, softened

1 cup granulated sugar

⅔ cup firmly packed light brown sugar

1 teaspoon almond extract

½ teaspoon vanilla extract

2 large eggs

1 cup semisweet chocolate morsels

1 cup dried tart cherries

🍫 DIRECTIONS

1. Sift flour, cocoa, baking soda, and salt together in a large bowl. Stir in toffee pieces and toss well; set aside.

2. In a large bowl with an electric mixer on medium-high speed, beat butter until creamy, about 2 minutes. Add granulated sugar and brown sugar gradually, beating until light and fluffy, about 3 minutes, and scraping down bowl once or twice. Beat in extracts, then eggs, one at a time, scraping down bowl. Add about one-third of flour mixture and mix on low speed. Gradually add remaining flour mixture, mixing just until blended. Stir in chocolate morsels and cherries. Cover with plastic wrap and chill dough at least 2 hours or overnight.

3. Preheat oven to 350°F. Line 2 cookie sheets with parchment paper.

4. Drop chilled dough by generously rounded tablespoon 2 inches apart on prepared cookie sheets. Bake until dry to touch but still a bit soft, about 12 minutes. Place sheets on racks and let cookies cool completely.

Chocolate Almond Sparkles

🍫 **TYPE** *Shaped cookie*

🍫 **DESCRIPTION** *Get ready for an amazing, chocolate truffle-like experience! These flourless cookies are deceptively plain looking. They look like a chocolate cookie rolled in sugar, but they are moist and elegant with an elusive honey and almond flavor. If you like dark chocolate, you will love these. I make them with Scharffen Berger 70 percent bittersweet chocolate; other chocolates might work, but the results will be different.*

🍫 **FIELD NOTES** *While in Vancouver I stumbled upon SEN5ES bakery. At first I was drawn to the chocolate truffles. But there, upon the counter, were these chocolate cookies wrapped up in a clear cellophane bag. They didn't look very exciting, but they were heralded as "The World's Best Cookie," so how could I resist? Thomas Haas is the creator and the bakery was nice enough to give me the recipe. I have tinkered with it a tad and added the chocolate shavings. (Haas, by the way, likes to use blackberry honey. Visit his locations in Toronto as well.)*

🍫 **LIFESPAN** *3 days at room temperature in airtight container*

Yield: *45 cookies*

🍫 INGREDIENTS

9 ounces Scharffen Berger 70 percent bittersweet chocolate, finely chopped

3 tablespoons unsalted butter, softened

2 large eggs

½ cup granulated sugar, plus more for rolling

1 tablespoon light-colored and -flavored honey, such as acacia, clover, or blackberry

¼ cup finely ground blanched almonds

1 tablespoon Dutch-processed unsweetened cocoa powder, sifted

Pinch of salt

🍫 DIRECTIONS

1. Set aside about ¼ cup (1 ounce) of the chopped chocolate. Melt remaining 8 ounces in top of double boiler over gently simmering water or in a bowl in a microwave. Remove from heat and gently stir in pieces of butter until butter becomes incorporated and mixture is smooth. Let cool slightly.

2. In a large bowl with an electric mixer on medium-high speed, beat eggs until thickened. Gradually add sugar and honey; increase speed to high and beat until a thick ribbon forms when you dribble the mixture back on itself. Don't rush this stage; it might take a few minutes.

3. Fold melted chocolate into the egg mixture by hand, then fold in ground nuts, cocoa, salt, and reserved chopped chocolate. Cover with plastic wrap and chill dough until firm enough to roll, at least 4 hours or overnight.

4. Preheat oven to 325°F. Line 2 cookie sheets with parchment paper.

5. Roll chilled dough between your palms into 1¼-inch balls. Do this quickly and with a light touch to prevent sticking. Place 2 inches apart on prepared cookie sheets. Gently flatten just enough so they won't roll off sheet. Meanwhile, place some granulated sugar in a small bowl to roll cookies in after they are baked. Bake until tops are dry but centers are still soft, about 12 minutes. If you try to gently lift the cookies, they should come away from the paper.

6. Place sheets on racks to cool for 5 minutes, during which time they will firm up. Now place cookies, one at a time, in bowl with sugar and very gently turn them around in sugar to coat. Place cookies directly on racks to cool completely.

Chocolate Chip Cherry Mandelbrot

🍫 **TYPE** *Shaped cookie*

. . . .

🍫 **DESCRIPTION** *Featuring the luscious combination of dark chocolate and cherries, these cookies look like biscotti, but are softer and richer because of the added butter. Like biscotti, they are shaped in a log, baked, sliced, and baked again.*

. . . .

🍫 **FIELD NOTES** *Mandelbrot has its roots in Eastern Europe and usually contains almonds. This version is based on a recipe from my Aunt Estelle from Fort Lee, New Jersey. She uses slivered almonds. I added the miniature chocolate chips and dried sour cherries, as well as the cinnamon sugar topping, which is from her sister Tommy's recipe. (Yes, Tommy is my aunt's nickname.)*

. . . .

🍫 **LIFESPAN** *1 month at room temperature in airtight container*

Yield: *28 mandelbrot*

🍫 INGREDIENTS

Dough:
2½ cups all-purpose flour
1½ teaspoons baking powder
¼ cup (½ stick) unsalted butter, softened
¾ cup granulated sugar
1 teaspoon vanilla extract
3 large eggs

⅓ cup miniature semisweet chocolate morsels
⅓ cup slivered almonds
⅓ cup dried sour cherries, chopped

Topping:
¼ cup granulated sugar
1½ teaspoons ground cinnamon

🍫 DIRECTIONS

1. Preheat oven to 350°F. Line a cookie sheet with parchment paper.

2. Whisk flour and baking powder together in a medium-size bowl.

3. In a large bowl with an electric mixer on medium-high speed, beat butter until creamy, about 2 minutes. Add sugar gradually, beating until light and fluffy, about 3 minutes, and scraping down bowl once or twice. Beat in vanilla, then eggs, scraping down bowl. Add about one-third of flour mixture and mix on low speed. Gradually add remaining flour mixture, mixing just until blended. Stir in chocolate morsels, nuts, and cherries. Prepare topping by stirring together sugar and cinnamon; set aside.

4. Using well-floured hands, divide dough in half and shape each piece by hand directly on cookie sheet into long, flat logs about 2 inches wide and 13 inches long.

5. Bake until slightly puffed, dry to touch, and light golden brown around edges and over top, about 30 minutes; bottoms will be an even medium brown.

Remove from oven and let cool 2 minutes by setting sheet on rack.

6. Gently remove each log from the pan and place on a cutting board. Diagonally cut mandelbrot into ¾-inch-thick slices, making cookies about 4 inches long. Place slices back on sheet, broad cut side down, spacing about ⅛ inch apart if you can. They might be touching, which is okay. The sheet will be crowded, but they will fit. Sprinkle with half the cinnamon sugar. Bake 5 minutes, flip them over, sprinkle with remaining cinnamon sugar, and bake until dry on surface but still a little soft if pressed, about 5 minutes more. Slide parchment onto racks to cool cookies completely.

Good Cookie Tip

There are different types of dried cherries available. Make sure to use tart or sour cherries that are slightly sweetened. Dried Bing or naturally sweet cherries will not give the same results.

Chocolate Chip Malted Milk Ball Cookies

🍫 **TYPE** *Drop cookie*

🍫 **DESCRIPTION** *The distinctive flavor of malt gives these cookies a twist. Malt powder as well as malted milk balls are added to the dough along with chocolate chips.*

🍫 **FIELD NOTES** *Ovaltine, the popular milk flavoring, is easy to find and adds an elusive malt flavor to these cookies. You can find it in any supermarket near the chocolate syrup and instant cocoa mixes.*

🍫 **LIFESPAN** *1 week at room temperature in airtight container*

Yield: *60 cookies*

🍫 INGREDIENTS

2¼ cups all-purpose flour
½ cup Ovaltine
1 teaspoon baking soda
1 teaspoon salt
1 cup (2 sticks) unsalted butter, softened
¾ cup granulated sugar

¾ cup firmly packed light brown sugar
1 teaspoon vanilla extract
2 large eggs
2 cups roughly crushed chocolate-covered malted milk balls (such as Whoppers)
1 cup semisweet chocolate morsels

🍫 DIRECTIONS

1. Whisk flour, Ovaltine, baking soda, and salt together in a small bowl.

2. In a large bowl with an electric mixer on medium-high speed, beat butter until creamy, about 2 minutes. Add granulated sugar and brown sugar gradually, beating until light and fluffy, about 3 minutes, and scraping down bowl once or twice. Beat in vanilla, then eggs, one at a time, scraping down bowl. Add about one-third of flour mixture and mix on low speed. Gradually add remaining flour mixture, mixing just until blended. Stir in crushed malted milk balls and chocolate morsels. Cover with plastic wrap and chill dough at least 2 hours or overnight.

3. Preheat oven to 375°F. Line 2 cookie sheets with parchment paper.

4. Drop chilled dough by generously rounded tablespoon 2 inches apart on prepared cookie sheets. Bake until edges and tops just begin to turn light golden brown, about 12 minutes. Place sheets on racks to cool for 5 minutes, then remove cookies from sheets and place directly on racks to cool completely.

Good Cookie Tip

The chocolate-covered malted milk balls that I purchased came in a bag. I rolled a rolling pin over the bag before opening it to simply, and cleanly, crush the candies.

Chocolate Chip
Peanut Butter Hills

🍫 **TYPE** *Drop cookie*

🍫 **DESCRIPTION** *These begin with chocolate chip cookie dough, but a little bit of peanut butter is added, resulting in a wonderful flavor and texture. Semisweet chocolate and peanut butter morsels are folded in and the baked and cooled cookies are drizzled with a fudge frosting. A candy thermometer is helpful for making the frosting.*

🍫 **FIELD NOTES** *These cookies were developed by my friend Chelsea Brown, an amazing baker, who just happened to be 15 years old when she gave me this recipe. I have known her since before she was born, as the saying goes, and whenever there is a party, she and I are the ones bringing dessert! She has been baking for years and I cannot wait to see what else she comes up with. She and her mom, Claudia, named these cookies "hills" not only because they come out in little mounded shapes, but because they live on Butterhill Road. No wonder Chelsea is a baker! The techniques featured are as suggested by Chelsea.*

🍫 **LIFESPAN** *1 week at room temperature in airtight container in single layers separated by waxed (or parchment) paper*

Yield: *24 cookies*

🍫 INGREDIENTS

Cookies:

6 tablespoons (¾ stick) unsalted butter or margarine

2 tablespoons hydrogenated peanut butter, smooth or chunky (don't use natural)

½ cup firmly packed light brown sugar

¼ cup granulated sugar

¼ teaspoon baking soda

1 large egg

1 teaspoon vanilla extract

1¼ cups all-purpose flour

1 cup semisweet chocolate morsels

½ cup peanut butter morsels

Frosting:

2 ounces semisweet chocolate, finely chopped

½ teaspoon unsalted butter

⅓ cup granulated sugar

2 tablespoons water

🍫 DIRECTIONS

1. Preheat oven to 375°F. Have 2 cookie sheets ready (Chelsea uses them ungreased; you can line them with parchment paper if you like).

2. In a large bowl with an electric mixer on medium-high speed, beat butter and peanut butter together until creamy, about 2 minutes. Add brown sugar and granulated sugar gradually, beating until light and fluffy, about 3 minutes, and scraping down bowl once or twice. Beat in baking soda, then egg and vanilla. Add about one-third of the flour and mix on low speed. Gradually add the remaining flour, mixing just until blended. Stir in both morsels. Drop by generously rounded tablespoon 2 inches apart on prepared cookie sheets.

3. Bake until edges and tops just begin to turn light golden brown, about 12 minutes. Place sheets on racks to cool for 5 minutes, then remove cookies from sheets and place directly on racks to cool completely.

4. To make frosting, melt chocolate and butter together in medium-size saucepan over low heat or in a bowl in a microwave; stir until smooth and set aside. Combine granulated sugar and water in a small, heavy saucepan; stir to wet sugar. Bring to a boil over medium-high heat, swirling pan occasionally. Cook until it reaches 230°F on a candy thermometer, the thread stage (this means that when you drizzle a little of it in cold water, it will spin a thread in the water). Slowly pour the sugar syrup over the melted chocolate, whisking constantly. Initially the chocolate might look like it has seized; just keep whisking until completely smooth. Immediately drizzle the fudge frosting over the cookies; just dip a spoon in the frosting and make zigzag motions over the cookies.

Chocolate Chip Pizza Cookie

🍫 TYPE *Shaped cookie*

🍫 DESCRIPTION *This "pizza" begins with a crust of chocolate chip cookie dough that is baked into a 12-inch round. Then you spread the baked cookie with raspberry jam and sprinkle it with white chocolate "cheese." Seedless jam looks a little more like tomato sauce, but jam with seeds is just fine. To make the "cheese," grate the white chocolate on the largest holes of a box grater. Start with a chunky piece of bulk chocolate, which is easiest to hold and grate. Cut the "pizza" into wedges to serve.*

🍫 FIELD NOTES *In malls throughout America, chocolate chip cookie stores feature huge, platter-sized cookies. They are very popular for kids' birthday parties and, I figured, there is no reason you cannot do these at home.*

🍫 RELATED SPECIES *Instead of topping the giant cookie with jam and chocolate "cheese," you can write the name of a friend on the cookie with melted chocolate in a zipper-lock plastic bag (see page 49). These are great for birthday "cakes" or whenever you want to relay a message: Get Well, Congratulations, what have you. For Valentine's Day, make the cookie heart-shaped and write…well, write whatever you like!*

🍫 LIFESPAN *3 days at room temperature in airtight container*

Yield: *1 pizza cookie*

🍫 INGREDIENTS

1¼ cups all-purpose flour
½ teaspoon salt
½ teaspoon baking soda
½ cup (1 stick) unsalted butter, softened
⅓ cup granulated sugar
⅓ cup firmly packed light brown sugar
½ teaspoon vanilla extract
1 large egg

¼ cup miniature semisweet chocolate morsels
½ cup raspberry jam, preferably seedless
1 ounce white chocolate, grated (see Description, page 64)
1 tablespoon milk chocolate morsels (optional)
1 tablespoon peanut butter morsels (optional)

🍫 DIRECTIONS

1. Line 1 cookie sheet with parchment paper (make sure the sheet is at least 12 inches wide).

2. Whisk flour, salt, and baking soda together in a small bowl.

3. In a large bowl with an electric mixer on medium-high speed, beat butter until creamy, about 2 minutes. Add granulated sugar and brown sugar gradually, beating until light and fluffy, about 3 minutes, and scraping down bowl once or twice. Beat in vanilla, then egg. Add about one-third of flour mixture and mix on low speed. Gradually add remaining flour mixture, mixing just until blended. Stir in miniature morsels. Pat dough with floured fingertips into a 12-inch round on prepared cookie sheet. Flour your palms and flatten and smooth out the "pizza" as evenly as possible. Cover with plastic wrap and chill at least 1 hour or overnight.

4. Preheat oven to 350°F, then bake until edges and top are light golden brown, about 15 minutes. Place pan on rack to cool "pizza" completely.

5. Spread jam over cooled cookie, leaving a ½-inch border all around edge. Sprinkle with white chocolate "cheese," then sprinkle with milk chocolate and peanut butter morsels, if using, for the look of additional "toppings." Cut into wedges to serve.

Good Cookie Tip

You can use a 12-inch pot or pan as a guide for your "pizza." Just place the pot on the parchment and trace a circle with a pen. Flip the parchment over before placing it on your cookie sheet so that no ink will get on your "pizza"!

Chocolate Chocolate Chip Shortbread

TYPE *Shaped cookie*

DESCRIPTION *These taste as dark and chocolatey as they look. A very rich cocoa-enhanced shortbread cookie dough is rolled into a ball and the top is dipped into and covered with chocolate morsels. These easy-to-make cookies are almost 3 inches across and look kind of fancy–though not dainty!*

FIELD NOTES *I used to make these at my bakery, Harvest Moon, in Amherst, Massachusetts, all the time. They were developed to satisfy any dark chocolate craving.*

RELATED SPECIES *Some folks like the deep cocoa flavor of this dough so much that they would prefer it with less chips. Sometimes I use only 1 cup semisweet chocolate morsels and stir them in right after adding the flour. Then scoop and bake as directed.*

LIFESPAN *2 weeks at room temperature in airtight container*

Yield: *21 cookies*

🍫 INGREDIENTS

3½ cups all-purpose flour

1 cup plus 3 tablespoons Dutch-processed unsweetened cocoa powder

2 cups (4 sticks) unsalted butter, softened

2½ cups confectioners' sugar

2 tablespoons vanilla extract

1½ cups semisweet chocolate morsels

🍫 DIRECTIONS

1. Preheat oven to 350°F. Line 2 cookie sheets with parchment paper.

2. Whisk flour and cocoa together in a large bowl.

3. In another large bowl with an electric mixer on medium-high speed, beat butter until creamy, about 2 minutes. Add confectioners' sugar, beating until light and fluffy, about 3 minutes, and scraping down bowl once or twice. Beat in vanilla. Add about one-third of flour mixture and mix on low speed. Gradually add remaining flour mixture, mixing just until blended. Place chocolate morsels in a small bowl.

4. Use a ¼-cup measuring cup to form portions of dough. Roll each cookie into a ball and press one side into the chocolate morsels so that they stick well. Place 2 inches apart on prepared cookie sheets, morsel side up. Flatten each one, using your palm, to ½-inch thickness (they will be about 2¾ inches across after flattening).

5. Bake until dry to the touch, about 25 minutes. They will not brown but you should be able to lift them gently from parchment paper with a metal spatula without breaking. Slide parchment onto racks to cool cookies completely.

Chocolate-Flecked Almond Drops

🍫 **TYPE** *Shaped cookie*

🍫 **DESCRIPTION** *Almond paste gives these cookies an unmistakable moist almond flavor. The chocolate chips in this cookie are chopped bittersweet chocolate.*

🍫 **FIELD NOTES** *Specialty food stores will have the highest-quality almond paste. If you buy yours in the supermarket, buy the canned type, not the kind in the tube, as it has the better texture and flavor. For maximum chocolate impact, dip the baked and cooled cookies halfway into tempered chocolate, page 14.*

🍫 **LIFESPAN** *1 week at room temperature in airtight container*

Yield: *34 cookies*

🍫 INGREDIENTS

½ pound canned almond paste
¾ cup plus 1 tablespoon granulated sugar
2 large egg whites

⅓ cup chopped bittersweet chocolate
(⅛-inch with some slivers), about
1½ ounces
1 cup sliced almonds

🍫 DIRECTIONS

1. Preheat oven to 350°F. Line 2 cookie sheets with parchment paper.

2. In a large bowl with an electric mixer on medium-high speed, beat almond paste and sugar together until creamy, about 2 minutes. Add egg whites and beat on medium speed until smooth, about 2 minutes, scraping down bowl once or twice. Fold in chopped chocolate.

3. Place almonds in a shallow dish, such as a pie plate. Roll dough between your palms into 1-inch balls. Roll balls around in almonds to coat completely and place on prepared cookie sheet 2 inches apart.

4. Bake until light golden brown around edges, puffed, and pale gold on top, about 15 minutes. Slide parchment onto racks to cool cookies completely.

Good Cookie Tip

Once I made these on a very humid day and they took a full 5 minutes longer to bake. Always use the visual cues given in the recipe as your ultimate guide to doneness.

Chocolate Pistachio Biscotti

🍫 **TYPE** *Shaped cookie*

🍫 **DESCRIPTION** *These are rich, full of cocoa and chocolate, and studded with pale green pistachios.*

🍫 **FIELD NOTES** *Sometimes biscotti seem like a healthy cookie because they are dry and crisp and seem somewhat austere. These biscotti are luxurious and decadent. Use a high-quality bittersweet chocolate for the best results. To really gild the lily, temper chocolate as described on page 14 and dip the baked biscotti halfway diagonally into the chocolate. Place on a parchment-lined pan and refrigerate until chocolate is set.*

🍫 **RELATED SPECIES** Chocolate-Covered Almond Biscotti: *Go to a candy or specialty store and buy cocoa-dusted chocolate-covered almonds. Roughly chop them and use them in place of the pistachios. Yum!*

🍫 **LIFESPAN** *2 weeks at room temperature in airtight container*

Yield: *45 biscotti*

🍫 INGREDIENTS

4¼ cups all-purpose flour
¼ cup Dutch-processed unsweetened
  cocoa powder
1 tablespoon baking powder
1 teaspoon salt
4 ounces bittersweet chocolate, finely
  chopped
1 cup (2 sticks) unsalted butter, softened
¾ cup granulated sugar
¾ cup lightly packed light brown sugar
1 teaspoon almond extract
1 teaspoon vanilla extract
4 large eggs

1½ cups bittersweet chocolate chunks
  (¼-inch), about 7½ ounces
1½ cups shelled unsalted natural
  pistachios, toasted (see page 16) and
  roughly chopped

Good Cookie Tip

Pistachios come in their natural state, which is undyed and a pretty pale green, and then there are those bright red ones, which are full of unnecessary coloring. Please search out the green ones. If you can only find salted ones, place them in a strainer, rinse under cool water, and pat dry with a clean towel.

🍫 DIRECTIONS

1. Preheat oven to 325°F. Line 2 cookie sheets with parchment paper.

2. Sift flour, cocoa, baking powder, and salt together in a large bowl.

3. Melt bittersweet chocolate in top of double boiler set over gently simmering water or in a bowl in a microwave. Stir until smooth, then let cool slightly.

4. In another large bowl with an electric mixer on medium-high speed, beat butter until creamy, about 2 minutes. Add granulated sugar and brown sugar gradually, beating until light and fluffy, about 3 minutes, and scraping down bowl once or twice. Beat in both extracts, then eggs, one at a time, allowing each one to be absorbed before adding the next. Beat in melted chocolate. Add about one-third of flour mixture and mix on low speed. Gradually add remaining flour mixture, mixing just until blended. Stir in chocolate chunks and nuts.

5. Form four logs (two on each sheet). They should be almost the length of the pan, leaving about 2 inches at either end, and about 2 inches wide. Batter will be wet but firm; use floured hands to help roll them into shape.

6. Bake until tops and sides are dry and firm, about 30 minutes. Center will still have some spring to it. Remove from oven, place sheets on racks, and let cool for 10 minutes.

7. Place logs on cutting surface and cut diagonally into ½-inch-thick slices. Place slices back on sheets, broad cut side down, spacing about ¼ inch apart. Bake 5 minutes, flip over, and bake until dry, about 5 minutes more. Remove cookies from sheets and place directly on racks to cool completely.

Chocolate Polka-Dot Mint Crackles

🍫 **TYPE** *Shaped cookie*

🍫 **DESCRIPTION** *These chocolate cookies develop an interesting crackled appearance while baking and need no further embellishment; they will look at home on the fanciest cookie tray. They are dotted with white chocolate chips, hence the "polka dot" name.*

🍫 **FIELD NOTES** *Use Frontier brand mint flavoring for the purest mint taste. A combination of pure peppermint oil and a flavorless oil base, it is stronger and cleaner tasting than mint extract. Peppermint extract cannot be substituted.*

🍫 **RELATED SPECIES** Chocolate Polka-Dot Crackles: *Substitute vanilla extract for the mint flavoring;* Chocolate Orange Polka-Dot Crackles: *Substitute vanilla extract for the mint flavoring and add 2 teaspoons grated orange zest to the sugar-egg mixture;* Chocolate Cinnamon Polka-Dot Crackles: *Add ½ teaspoon ground cinnamon and substitute vanilla extract for the mint flavoring.*

🍫 **LIFESPAN** *2 weeks at room temperature in airtight container in single layers separated by waxed (or parchment) paper*

Yield: *60 cookies*

◆ INGREDIENTS

5 ounces unsweetened chocolate, finely chopped
½ cup (1 stick) unsalted butter, cut into tablespoons
2 cups all-purpose flour
2 teaspoons baking powder
¼ teaspoon salt

4 large eggs
2 cups granulated sugar, plus more for rolling in
1 teaspoon mint flavoring (see Field Notes, page 72)
¾ cup white chocolate morsels
Confectioners' sugar

◆ DIRECTIONS

1. Melt chocolate and butter together in a medium-size saucepan over low heat or in a bowl in a microwave until about three-quarters melted. Remove from heat and stir until completely melted and smooth.

2. Meanwhile, whisk flour, baking powder, and salt together in a medium-size bowl.

3. In a large bowl with an electric mixer on high speed, beat eggs, 2 cups granulated sugar, and mint flavoring together on high speed until thick and creamy, about 2 minutes. Whisk chocolate-butter mixture until smooth, then beat into egg mixture until entire mixture is smooth, scraping down bowl once or twice. Add about one-third of flour mixture and mix on low speed. Gradually add remaining flour, mixing just until blended, scraping down bowl. Stir in chocolate morsels. Dough may be very thin; that's okay because it will firm up upon cooling. Cover with plas-

tic wrap and chill dough until firm enough to roll, at least 6 hours or overnight.

4. Preheat oven to 350°F. Line 2 cookie sheets with parchment paper.

5. Place some granulated sugar in a small bowl and sift some confectioners' sugar into another small bowl.

6. Roll chilled dough between your palms into 1-inch balls. Roll each ball first in granulated sugar, then in confectioners' sugar to coat completely. Place balls on prepared cookie sheets 2 inches apart and gently flatten just enough so they won't roll off.

7. Bake until puffed, crackled in appearance, and surface is dry to touch, about 12 minutes; centers will still feel somewhat soft. You should be able to gently lift edge of a cookie up from parchment with a metal spatula. Slide parchment onto racks to cool cookies completely.

Chunky Chocolate Chipsters

🍫 **TYPE** *Drop cookie*

🍫 **DESCRIPTION** *A dark cocoa-enhanced dough is filled with raisins and peanuts, just like a Chunky candy bar.*

🍫 **FIELD NOTES** *Have you ever had a Chunky? It is a chocolate bar shaped like a chunky cube filled with raisins and peanuts. This classic combination lent itself perfectly to a cookie with added morsels.*

🍫 **LIFESPAN** *1 week at room temperature in airtight container*

Yield: *60 cookies*

🍫 INGREDIENTS

2¼ cups all-purpose flour
¼ cup Dutch-processed unsweetened
  cocoa powder
1 teaspoon baking soda
½ teaspoon salt
1 cup (2 sticks) unsalted butter, softened
1 cup firmly packed dark brown sugar

¾ cup granulated sugar
1 teaspoon vanilla extract
2 large eggs
2 cups semisweet chocolate morsels
1 cup salted dry-roasted peanuts
1 cup dark raisins

🍫 DIRECTIONS

1. Whisk flour, cocoa powder, baking soda, and salt together in a medium-size bowl.

2. In a large bowl with an electric mixer on medium-high speed, beat butter until creamy, about 2 minutes. Add brown sugar and granulated sugar gradually, beating until light and fluffy, about 3 minutes, and scraping down bowl once or twice. Beat in vanilla, then eggs, one at a time, scraping down bowl. Add about one-third of flour mixture and mix on low speed. Gradually add remaining flour mixture, mixing just until blended. Stir in chocolate morsels, peanuts, and raisins.

Cover with plastic wrap and chill dough at least 2 hours or overnight.

3. Preheat oven to 375°F. Line 2 cookie sheets with parchment paper.

4. Drop chilled dough by generously rounded tablespoon 2 inches apart on prepared cookie sheets. Bake until firmed up but still a bit soft in center, about 10 minutes. Place sheets on racks to cool for 5 minutes, then remove cookies from sheets and place directly on racks to cool completely.

Good Cookie Tip

If you'd like, use chocolate-covered peanuts and raisins to up the chocolate quotient.

Cinnamon Oatmeal Chocolate Chip Cookies

TYPE *Drop cookie*

DESCRIPTION *This cookie is halfway between a regular chocolate chip cookie and a typical oatmeal cookie; it combines oats and cinnamon in a chocolate chip cookie dough.*

FIELD NOTES *I have found that the strength of cinnamon can vary widely. This recipe is supposed to have a real cinnamon kick. If your cinnamon isn't pungent, add a little extra.*

LIFESPAN *1 week at room temperature in airtight container*

Yield: *48 cookies*

◗ INGREDIENTS

2½ cups oats (use old-fashioned, not quick or instant)

1½ cups all-purpose flour

1 teaspoon baking soda

1 teaspoon ground cinnamon

½ teaspoon salt

1 cup (2 sticks) unsalted butter, softened

⅔ cup firmly packed light brown sugar

⅔ cup firmly packed dark brown sugar

1 teaspoon vanilla extract

2 large eggs

1 cup semisweet chocolate morsels

⅔ cup walnut halves, toasted (see page 16) and chopped

◗ DIRECTIONS

1. Whisk oats, flour, baking soda, cinnamon, and salt together in a large bowl.

2. In another large bowl with an electric mixer on medium-high speed, beat butter until creamy, about 2 minutes. Add brown sugars gradually, beating until light and fluffy, about 3 minutes, scraping down bowl once or twice. Beat in vanilla, then eggs, one at a time, scraping down bowl. Add about one-third of flour mixture and mix on low speed. Gradually add remaining flour mixture, mixing just until blended. Stir in chocolate morsels and nuts. Cover with plastic wrap and chill dough at least 2 hours or overnight.

3. Preheat oven to 325°F. Line 2 cookie sheets with parchment paper.

4. Drop chilled dough by generously rounded tablespoon 2 inches apart on prepared cookie sheets; flatten cookies using your floured palm to about ¾-inch thickness. Bake until edges and tops just begin to turn light golden brown, about 11 minutes. Cookies will be a bit darker and firmer around edges, but soft on top. Place sheets on racks to cool for 5 minutes, then remove cookies from sheets and place directly on racks to cool completely.

Classic Toll House Cookies

🍫 **TYPE** *Drop cookie*

🍫 **DESCRIPTION** *Both chewy and crispy with a buttery brown sugar flavor, these are the standard against which most chocolate chip cookies are judged. There is a nice balance between cookie dough and chips (not too much or too little of either) and they also feature a scattering of chopped nuts.*

🍫 **FIELD NOTES** *Ruth and Kenneth Wakefield bought a Cape Cod–style house in Whitman, Massachusetts, in 1930 and promptly turned it into an inn and restaurant. In decades past the building had served as a toll house, where travelers could rest and pay any accompanying tolls, hence they named their place The Toll House. Ruth was responsible for the recipes whipped up in the kitchen. The story goes that she was making cookies, chopped up a chocolate candy bar, and added it to the dough, thinking it would melt and she would have chocolate cookies. Well, the rest is history. The chunks did not melt and the delectable chocolate chip cookie was born. In 1939 Nestlé bought the rights to the recipe and began selling the chocolate "morsels" we all know and love with the recipe right on the package. The ingredients in this recipe are the same as the ones in the 1947 edition of* Ruth Wakefield's Toll House Tried and True Recipes

(M. Barrows & Co., Inc., New York), where they were called Toll House Chocolate Crunch Cookies. Ruth liked them tiny and dropped them by the half-teaspoon. Here they are a bit larger.

🍫 **RELATED SPECIES** *All the cookies in this book! The original Toll House cookie showed us that chocolate chips and chunks could retain their shape and add a delicious dimension to our cookie recipes.*

🍫 **LIFESPAN** *1 week at room temperature in airtight container*

Yield: *50 cookies*

🍫 **INGREDIENTS**

2¼ cups all-purpose flour
I teaspoon salt
I cup (2 sticks) unsalted butter, softened
¾ cup granulated sugar
¾ cup firmly packed light brown sugar
I teaspoon vanilla extract

2 large eggs
I teaspoon baking soda
I teaspoon hot water
2 cups plus 2 tablespoons Nestlé semisweet chocolate morsels
I cup walnut or pecan halves, chopped

🍫 **DIRECTIONS**

1. Preheat oven to 375°F. Have 2 cookie sheets ready (you will use them as is, ungreased).

2. Stir flour and salt together in a medium-size bowl.

3. In a large bowl with an electric mixer on medium-high speed, beat butter until creamy, about 2 minutes. Add granulated sugar and brown sugar gradually, beating until light and fluffy, about 3 minutes, and scraping down bowl once or twice. Beat in vanilla, then eggs, one at a time, scraping down bowl. Dissolve baking soda in hot water and beat into cookie mixture on low speed. Add about one-third of flour mixture and mix on low speed. Gradually add remaining flour mixture, mixing just until blended. Stir in chocolate morsels and nuts. Drop by generously rounded tablespoon 2 inches apart on cookie sheets.

4. Bake until edges and tops just begin to turn light golden brown, about 10 minutes. Place sheets on racks to cool for 5 minutes, then remove cookies from sheets and place directly on racks to cool completely. Or, eat them warm!

Clipper Chippers

🍫 **TYPE** *Drop cookie*

🍫 **DESCRIPTION** *These cookies are absolutely jam-packed with goodies. A luscious dough flavored with Tia Maria coffee liqueur and Frangelico hazelnut liqueur is chock-full of milk chocolate morsels, toasted pecans, walnuts, and buttery macadamias.*

🍫 **FIELD NOTES** *Clipper Cruise Line offers small-ship travel the world over and on every ship at 4:30 in the afternoon, a platter of these cookies, warm from the oven, is offered to guests. Their chefs say that the overnight chilling allows the flavors of the liqueurs to permeate the dough. It is their most requested recipe and has been featured in* Bon Appétit *magazine.*

🍫 **LIFESPAN** *1 week at room temperature in airtight container*

Yield: *64 cookies*

🍫 INGREDIENTS

2½ cups all-purpose flour
1 teaspoon baking soda
½ teaspoon salt
1 cup (2 sticks) unsalted butter, softened
¾ cup granulated sugar
¾ cup firmly packed light brown sugar
1 tablespoon vanilla extract

1 tablespoon Tia Maria liqueur
1 tablespoon Frangelico liqueur
2 large eggs
4 cups milk chocolate morsels
1 cup walnut halves, toasted (see page 16)
½ cup pecan halves, toasted (see page 16)
½ cup macadamias, toasted (see page 16)

🍫 DIRECTIONS

1. Whisk flour, baking soda, and salt together in a medium-size bowl.

2. In a large bowl with an electric mixer on medium-high speed, beat butter until creamy, about 2 minutes. Add granulated sugar and brown sugar gradually, beating until light and fluffy, about 3 minutes, and scraping down bowl once or twice. Beat in vanilla and liqueurs, then eggs, one at a time, scraping down bowl. Add about one-third of flour mixture and mix on low speed. Gradually add remaining flour mixture, mixing just until blended. Stir in chocolate morsels and nuts. Cover with plastic wrap and chill dough at least overnight or up to 4 days.

3. Preheat oven to 325°F. Line 2 cookie sheets with parchment paper.

4. Drop chilled dough by generously rounded tablespoon 2 inches apart on prepared cookie sheets. Flatten slightly to scant 1-inch thickness. Bake until light golden brown all over, but still soft, about 15 minutes. Place sheets on racks to cool cookies for about 2 minutes. Serve warm.

Coconut Chocolate Chip Snowballs

🍫 **TYPE** *Drop cookie*

🍫 **DESCRIPTION** *These are moist and coconut-y. If you like the texture and flavor of Mounds candy bars, which combine coconut and dark chocolate, then these are for you.*

🍫 **FIELD NOTES** *You need two kinds of coconut for this cookie. Look in natural food stores for the unsweetened coconut, which has a fine texture. The sweetened flaked coconut can be found in the supermarket.*

🍫 **LIFESPAN** *1 week at room temperature in airtight container in single layers separated by waxed (or parchment) paper*

Yield: *21 snowballs*

◕ INGREDIENTS

4 large egg whites
¾ cup granulated sugar
1 teaspoon vanilla extract
1½ cups unsweetened grated coconut
(5 ounces)

1½ cups sweetened flaked coconut
(4 ounces)
½ cup miniature semisweet chocolate
morsels

◕ DIRECTIONS

1. Preheat oven to 375°F. Line 2 cookie sheets with parchment paper; coat lightly with nonstick cooking spray.

2. Whisk together egg whites, sugar, and vanilla in top of a double boiler (not over hot water yet) until combined. Add both types of coconut and fold in until coconut is completely coated with egg white mixture. Place top of double boiler over simmering water with the water just touching the bottom of the part that is holding the cookie mixture. Stir constantly; the sugar will dissolve and mixture will become glossy and hot to touch in about 3 minutes.

Remove from simmering water, allow to cool slightly, and stir in chocolate morsels.

3. Drop 2-tablespoon-size mounds 2 inches apart on prepared cookie sheets. Cookies should be a rounded dome shape. Coax them into a neat shape with your fingers if needed by pressing any stray coconut shreds around edges into the cookie mound.

4. Bake until edges and some of the coconut shreds turn light golden brown, about 12 minutes. Slide parchment onto racks to cool cookies completely.

Coffee Toffee
Chocolate Chunk Cookies

🍫 **TYPE** *Drop cookie*

🍫 **DESCRIPTION** *Mmm-mmm. If you like coffee Heath Bar ice cream, you're gonna love this cookie. It may not be the prettiest one around, but it is rich and buttery, crumbly and satisfying. It is filled with coffee flavor in the dough, and packed with nuggets of Heath Bars and semisweet chocolate chunks.*

🍫 **FIELD NOTES** *This is one of my favorites! The melted white chocolate in the dough adds richness and is a perfect foil for the instant espresso powder dissolved in the vanilla. Big chunks of milk chocolate–covered toffee bars, such as Heath Bars, add buttery butterscotch flavor and crunchy texture. Semisweet chocolate chunks add a nice counterpoint.*

🍫 **LIFESPAN** *1 week at room temperature in airtight container*

Yield: *30 cookies*

♠ INGREDIENTS

3¾ cups all-purpose flour
½ teaspoon salt
4 ounces white chocolate (such as Callebaut or Ghirardelli), finely chopped
1½ cups (3 sticks) unsalted butter, softened
½ cup granulated sugar
½ cup firmly packed light brown sugar

1 tablespoon instant espresso powder
2 teaspoons vanilla extract
1¼ cups semisweet chocolate chunks (½-inch), about 6¼ ounces
Five 1.4-ounce milk chocolate–covered toffee bars, such as Heath Bars, chopped (½-inch)

♠ DIRECTIONS

1. Preheat oven to 325°F. Line 2 cookie sheets with parchment paper.

2. Whisk flour and salt together in a large bowl.

3. Melt white chocolate in top of double boiler over gently simmering water or in a bowl in a microwave. Stir until smooth and let cool.

4. In a large bowl with an electric mixer on medium-high speed, beat butter until creamy, about 2 minutes. Add granulated sugar and brown sugar gradually, beating until light and fluffy, about 3 minutes, and scraping down bowl once or twice. Dissolve instant espresso powder in vanilla, then beat into butter mixture. Beat in melted white chocolate. Add about one-third of flour mixture and mix on low speed. Gradually add remaining flour mixture, mixing just until blended. Stir in chocolate chunks and chopped toffee bars. Drop by generously rounded tablespoon 2 inches apart on prepared cookie sheets. Flatten cookies, using your palm, to about ½-inch thickness.

5. Bake until just beginning to turn light golden brown, about 20 minutes. Centers will still be a bit soft. Place sheets on racks to cool for 2 minutes, then remove cookies from sheets and place directly on racks to cool completely.

Cognac Apricot Rugelach with Mini-Chips

🍫 **TYPE** *Rolled and shaped cookie*

🍫 **DESCRIPTION** *These little crescents are filled with tart apricots plumped in cognac, walnuts, and mini semisweet chocolate chips. Most rugelach dough recipes use either cream cheese or sour cream; this one uses both with buttery, rich, flaky results. Also, this is one finished cookie that freezes pretty well; see Lifespan below.*

🍫 **FIELD NOTES** *Jams are very sweet. You could use apricot jam, but the 100 percent fruit spread is a better option. You can find it right next to the jams and jellies in any supermarket.*

🍫 **LIFESPAN** *4 days at room temperature in airtight container in single layers separated by waxed (or parchment) paper or frozen up to 1 month. To freeze, place rugelach on a cookie sheet and freeze, then pack frozen cookies in airtight plastic containers and slip those into zipper-lock plastic bags. To serve, defrost in refrigerator overnight and reheat in preheated 250°F oven.*

Yield: *48 rugelach*

🍫 INGREDIENTS

Dough:
4 cups all-purpose flour
¼ teaspoon salt
2 cups (4 sticks) unsalted butter, softened
One 8-ounce package cream cheese, softened
½ cup granulated sugar
½ cup sour cream
2 teaspoons vanilla extract

Filling:
1 cup (7 ounces) dried apricots
¼ cup cognac
½ cup granulated sugar
½ cup firmly packed light brown sugar

½ cup apricot fruit spread (100 percent fruit; no sugar added)
⅓ cup miniature semisweet chocolate chips
⅓ cup walnut halves, toasted (see page 16) and chopped

Topping:
¼ cup whole milk
¼ cup granulated sugar mixed with 2 teaspoons ground cinnamon

🍫 DIRECTIONS

1. Whisk flour and salt in a large bowl.

2. In a large bowl with an electric mixer on high speed, beat together butter and cream cheese until light and creamy, 3 to 5 minutes. Add granulated sugar gradually and beat until fluffy. Gently beat in sour cream and vanilla. Add flour mixture in 2 to 3 batches, beating until just combined.

3. Divide dough into quarters and wrap in plastic, shaping each into a flat, round disc. Chill 2 hours or overnight.

4. To make filling, place apricots and cognac in food processor and pulse until apricots are finely chopped. Scrape into large bowl and add remaining filling ingredients, stirring well to combine. (May be made 2 days ahead. Refrigerate in an airtight container.)

5. When ready, roll out each piece of chilled dough on a floured work board into an 8-inch circle about ⅛ inch thick (the thinness of the dough is what is important). Spread filling over dough thinly and evenly, going all the way to the edges. Using a sharp knife or a pizza cutter, divide each circle into 12 wedge-shaped pieces. Starting at the broad, outer edge, roll each piece up and place 2 inches apart on cookie sheets lined with parchment paper with center point underneath each rugelach. Shape gently into a crescent shape, if desired. Chill 30 minutes or cover with plastic wrap and chill overnight or up to 2 days.

6. Fifteen minutes before baking, preheat oven to 350°F. Brush chilled rugelach with milk and sprinkle with cinnamon sugar. Bake until puffed and very light golden brown, about 20 minutes. The bottoms burn easily, so be careful not to overbake. Place sheets on racks to cool for 5 minutes, then remove cookies from sheets and place directly on racks to cool completely.

Couture Chocolate
Fleur de Sel Cookies

🍫 **TYPE** *Shaped cookie*

. . . .

🍫 **DESCRIPTION** *These are elegant, buttery, deep, dark, and chocolatey with a textural surprise hit of salt—very haute couture and European.* Fleur de sel *has a crunchy texture and very pure flavor that is essential to this recipe. Also, the very bittersweet (70 percent) Valrhona Guanaja chocolate is integral to the grown-up flavor of the final result. Look for both in specialty food stores or through mail order.*

. . . .

🍫 **FIELD NOTES** *Dorie Greenspan and Pierre Hermé are two of the planet's most talented pastry chefs. This is their recipe; who am I to fuss with perfection? Well, I did add a tiny bit more salt on top of the cookies, otherwise, this is the Korova Cookie found in Dorie's* Paris Sweets: Great Recipes from the City's Best Pastry Shops *(Broadway Books, 2002).*

. . . .

🍫 **LIFESPAN** *2 weeks at room temperature in airtight container*

Yield: *34 cookies*

🔸 INGREDIENTS

1¼ cups all-purpose flour

⅓ cup Dutch-processed unsweetened cocoa powder

½ teaspoon baking soda

½ cup plus 3 tablespoons (1 stick plus 3 tablespoons) unsalted butter, softened

⅔ cup firmly packed light brown sugar

¼ cup granulated sugar

1 teaspoon *fleur de sel*

1 teaspoon vanilla extract

1 cup plus 1 tablespoon Valrhona Guanaja bittersweet chocolate, very finely chopped (about 5 ounces)

🔸 DIRECTIONS

1. Sift flour, cocoa, and baking soda together in a medium-size bowl.

2. In a large bowl with an electric mixer on medium-high speed, beat butter until creamy, about 2 minutes. Add brown sugar and granulated sugar gradually, beating until light and fluffy, about 3 minutes, and scraping down bowl once or twice. Beat in ½ teaspoon of the *fleur de sel* and the vanilla. Add about one-third of flour mixture and mix on low speed. Gradually add remaining flour mixture and the chocolate, mixing just until blended. Mixture will look crumbly.

3. Turn out onto work surface and bring together into a ball by pressing together with your palms. Divide dough in half and roll each half into a log about 8½ inches long and 1½ inches in diameter using your hands to form them. Wrap each log with plastic wrap and chill at least 1 hour or overnight.

4. Preheat oven to 325°F. Line 2 cookie sheets with parchment paper.

5. Slice chilled logs into ½-inch-thick cookies and place 1 inch apart on prepared cookie sheets. Sprinkle cookies with remaining ½ teaspoon salt; there will just be a few grains on top of each cookie. Bake until dry but still soft, about 12 minutes. Do not overbake. Place sheets on racks to cool for 5 minutes, then remove cookies from sheets and place directly on racks to cool completely.

Good Cookie Tip

When you slice the cookies off the log, you want them to be as round as possible. Use your hands to constantly reshape the logs into cylinders and, as you slice the cookies, press any ragged edges into the cookie if they crumble or become misshapen.

Cowboy Lollipop Chocolate Chip Saucer Cookies

🍫 **TYPE** *Drop cookie*

🍫 **DESCRIPTION** *The first two things you will notice about these cookies are that they are huge—saucer size—and they are baked onto lollipop sticks! Bite into one of these and you will find a little bit of everything: chocolate, raisins, granola, coconut, and nuts. Kids love them. You can order the lollipop sticks from Sweet Celebrations (see Resources) or try a local craft shop. If you follow the cooking temperature and time in the recipe, you will have no problem with baking the sticks.*

🍫 **FIELD NOTES** *The shared aspect of all "cowboy" cookie recipes seems to be lots of stuff—chocolate, oats, nuts, raisins, and often coconut. I used granola as a twist. They are also often made very large, which seems to appeal to kids—and kid-like adults.*

🍫 **LIFESPAN** *1 week at room temperature in airtight container*

Yield: *18 cookies*

◆ INGREDIENTS

2 cups all-purpose flour
1 teaspoon baking soda
1 teaspoon salt
1 cup sweetened flaked coconut
1½ cups semisweet chocolate chunks
  (½-inch), about 7 ½ ounces
¾ cup pecan halves, toasted (see page 16)
  and chopped

¾ cup granola
¾ cup dark raisins
1 cup (2 sticks) unsalted butter, melted
¾ cup firmly packed dark brown sugar
½ cup granulated sugar
1 teaspoon vanilla extract
2 large eggs
Eighteen 6½-inch-long lollipop sticks

◆ DIRECTIONS

1. Whisk flour, baking soda, and salt together in a large bowl. Stir in coconut, chocolate, nuts, granola, and raisins.

2. In another large bowl, whisk together melted butter, brown sugar, and granulated sugar. Whisk in vanilla, then eggs, one at a time, blending well. Make sure mixture cools to room temperature before adding flour mixture. Stir in flour mixture, mixing just until blended. Cover with plastic wrap and chill dough at least 2 hours or overnight.

3. Preheat oven to 325°F. Line 3 cookie sheets with parchment paper.

4. Place lollipop sticks on prepared cookie sheets, spaced apart. You will probably be able to fit about 6 cookies per sheet. Drop chilled dough by ¼-cup amounts centered right on top of each stick. Gently flatten to about ½ inch thick; cookies should be about 2 inches apart with the sticks centered in each cookie.

Bake only two sheets at a time. Chill additional cookie sheet in the meantime, if you have room in your refrigerator.

5. Bake until edges and tops just begin to turn light golden brown, about 18 minutes. Cookies will still be soft and moist, but will firm up upon cooling. Place sheets on racks to cool cookies completely.

Good Cookie Tip

You can wrap these individually in cellophane and tie a ribbon underneath the cookie. They make great party favors. You can even make these with kids at a party and send them home with the fruits of their labor.

Cranberry Walnut Toffee Chocolate Chip Bars

🍫 **TYPE** *Bar cookie*

🍫 **DESCRIPTION** *These buttery brown sugar bars are packed with dried cranberries, toasted walnuts, toffee bits, and semisweet chocolate morsels.*

🍫 **FIELD NOTES** *I found a recipe for cranberry-walnut bars in a cookbook by Elinor Klivans. The word butterscotch was in the title, which made me think of toffee, which was not in the original recipe. Elinor also used orange peel. I decided to leave that out and add chocolate! Her recipe is delicious, so I just tinkered with it a little bit to bring you these bars.*

🍫 **LIFESPAN** *1 week at room temperature in airtight container*

Yield: *16 bars*

● INGREDIENTS

1⅓ cups all-purpose flour
1 teaspoon baking powder
½ teaspoon salt
½ cup toffee bits (such as Skor)
½ cup semisweet chocolate morsels
½ cup sweetened dried cranberries
½ cup walnut halves, toasted (see
  page 16) and chopped

¾ cup (1½ sticks) unsalted butter,
  softened
¾ cup firmly packed light brown sugar
½ cup granulated sugar
1 teaspoon vanilla extract
2 large eggs

● DIRECTIONS

1. Preheat oven to 325°F. Coat a 9 x 13-inch baking pan with nonstick cooking spray.

2. Whisk flour, baking powder, and salt together in a small bowl; stir in toffee bits until coated. Set aside. Toss together morsels, cranberries, and nuts in another small bowl; set aside.

3. In a large bowl with an electric mixer on medium-high speed, beat butter until creamy, about 3 minutes. Add brown sugar and granulated sugar gradually and beat on high speed until light and fluffy, about 3 minutes, scraping down bowl once or twice. Beat in vanilla, then eggs, one at a time, scraping down bowl. Add about one-third of flour mixture and mix on low speed. Gradually add remaining flour mixture, mixing just until blended. Stir in half the chocolate morsel–cranberry mixture. Spread mixture evenly in prepared pan.

4. Bake until just turning light golden brown around edges and top, but not fully cooked, about 15 minutes. Scatter remaining morsel-cranberry mixture evenly over top, return to oven, and bake until a toothpick inserted in center comes out with just a few moist crumbs, about another 20 minutes. Place pan on rack to cool completely. Cut into 16 bars (4 x 4).

Double Butterscotch Chocolate Chip Brownies

🍫 **TYPE** *Bar cookie*

🍫 **DESCRIPTION** *These are a classic "blondie"-type brownie with extra molasses, for moistness and flavor, and filled with butterscotch, milk chocolate morsels, and walnuts.*

🍫 **FIELD NOTES** *These are a great bar to make for bake sales. They are easy to whip up, cut cleanly, and last several days because they are very moist.*

🍫 **LIFESPAN** *1 week at room temperature in airtight container in single layers separated by waxed (or parchment) paper*

Yield: *16 bars*

🍫 INGREDIENTS

1 cup all-purpose flour
½ cup (1 stick) unsalted butter, softened
1¼ cups firmly packed light brown sugar
1 tablespoon unsulfured molasses
1 teaspoon vanilla extract

2 large eggs
½ cup milk chocolate morsels
½ cup butterscotch morsels
½ cup walnut halves, toasted (see page 16) and chopped

🍫 DIRECTIONS

1. Preheat oven to 350°F. Coat a 9-inch square baking pan with nonstick cooking spray.

2. Whisk flour in a small bowl.

3. In a large bowl with an electric mixer on medium-high speed, beat butter until creamy, about 2 minutes. Add brown sugar gradually, beating until light and fluffy, about 3 minutes, and scraping down bowl once or twice. Beat in molasses and vanilla, then eggs, one at a time, scraping down bowl.

Add about one-third of flour mixture and mix on low speed. Gradually add remaining flour mixture, mixing just until blended. Stir in chocolate and butterscotch morsels and nuts. Spread evenly into prepared pan.

4. Bake until lightly browned and edges have begun to pull away from sides of pan, about 35 minutes. A toothpick inserted in center should come out with some moist crumbs clinging. Place pan on rack until cool. Cut into 16 bars (4 x 4).

Double Chip Browned-Butter Oat Scotchies

♦ **TYPE** *Drop cookie*

♦ **DESCRIPTION** *These are chewy and rich due to the browned butter and dark brown sugar. Butterscotch chips are added to the warm dough, where they melt and enrich the flavor and texture of the cookie. Then, after cooling, additional chips, this time semisweet chocolate, are folded in for a jolt of chocolate.*

♦ **FIELD NOTES** *Adding butterscotch chips to oatmeal cookies is nothing new, but the double dose technique of adding the chips in two stages was developed for this recipe—by mistake! I started to stir in the chips and they began melting. So I added some more and voilà, a new recipe! Also, browning the butter for oatmeal cookies is another idea I came up with to accentuate the toasty flavor of the oats.*

♦ **LIFESPAN** *1 week at room temperature in airtight container*

Yield: *48 cookies*

● INGREDIENTS

2½ cups oats (use old-fashioned, not quick or instant)

1½ cups all-purpose flour

1 teaspoon baking soda

½ teaspoon salt

1 cup (2 sticks) unsalted butter, softened

⅔ cup granulated sugar

⅔ cup firmly packed dark brown sugar

1 teaspoon vanilla extract

2 large eggs

½ cup butterscotch morsels

½ cup semisweet chocolate morsels

½ cup walnuts, toasted (see page 16) and chopped

● DIRECTIONS

1. Preheat oven to 325°F. Line 2 cookie sheets with parchment paper.

2. Whisk oats, flour, baking soda, and salt together in a large bowl.

3. Melt butter over medium heat in a large saucepan, then simmer over medium-low heat until browned, 3 to 5 minutes. The milk solids will turn golden brown; do not let them burn.

4. Remove from heat and whisk in both sugars until combined. Whisk in vanilla and eggs, one at a time, until smooth.

5. While mixture is still warm, quickly stir in oat mixture and butterscotch morsels. Gently stir until the warmth of the butter melts the chips and they blend with rest of ingredients. Allow mixture to cool (about 5 minutes), then stir in chocolate morsels and nuts. Drop by generously rounded table-spoon 2 inches apart on prepared cookie sheets.

6. Bake until light golden brown but still moist and chewy in center, about 12 minutes. Tops will be softer than edges.

7. Place sheets on racks to cool for 5 min-utes, then remove cookies from sheets and place directly on racks to cool completely.

Espresso Kahlúa Buttercream Chunk Bars

🍫 **TYPE** *Bar cookie*

🍫 **DESCRIPTION** *These blondies are chocolate and coffee rich! They start with a brown sugar dough filled with chocolate chunks and flavored with instant espresso powder. After they come out of the oven, they are brushed with Kahlúa. Then, a rich, creamy frosting, also flavored with espresso and Kahlúa, tops them off. You can serve them without the frosting as well.*

🍫 **FIELD NOTES** *I love Medaglia d'Oro instant espresso powder. It is strong and flavorful and it adds a great depth to "coffee" recipes. You can use regular instant coffee, but the flavor will be less pronounced.*

🍫 **LIFESPAN** *4 days at room temperature in airtight container in single layers separated by waxed (or parchment) paper*

Yield: *20 bars*

🍫 INGREDIENTS

Cookie:
1 cup all-purpose flour
Heaping ½ teaspoon baking powder
⅛ teaspoon salt
½ cup (1 stick) unsalted butter, melted
1 cup firmly packed light brown sugar
2 teaspoons instant espresso powder
1 teaspoon vanilla extract
1 large egg
¾ cup bittersweet or semisweet chocolate chunks (½-inch), about 3¾ ounces
1 tablespoon Kahlúa liqueur

Frosting:
6 tablespoons (¾ stick) unsalted butter, softened
1¾ cups plus 2 tablespoons confectioners' sugar
1 tablespoon plus 1 teaspoon milk
1 tablespoon plus 2 teaspoons Kahlúa liqueur
1½ teaspoons instant espresso powder

🍫 DIRECTIONS

1. Preheat oven to 350°F. Coat an 8-inch square baking pan with nonstick cooking spray.

2. Whisk flour, baking powder, and salt together in a small bowl.

3. In a large bowl, whisk together melted butter and brown sugar. Whisk in espresso powder, vanilla, and egg, blending well. Stir in flour mixture, mixing just until blended. Make sure mixture is cool, then stir in chocolate chunks. Spread evenly in prepared pan.

4. Bake until light golden brown, slightly puffed, and edges have begun to pull away from sides of pan, about 30 minutes. A toothpick inserted in center should come out with some moist crumbs clinging. Immediately brush top with Kahlúa. Place pan on rack to cool completely.

5. To make frosting, in a medium-size bowl with an electric mixer on medium-low speed, beat frosting ingredients together until it starts to become creamy. Increase speed to high and beat until light, creamy, and smooth, about 3 minutes. Spread frosting evenly over cooled brownies. Cut into 20 bars (5 x 4).

Espresso White Chocolate Chunk Cookies

🍫 **TYPE** *Drop cookie*

🍫 **DESCRIPTION** *Do you like coffee? Then make these right now! Here I present to you white chocolate chips and dark chocolate–covered espresso beans folded into a brown sugar dough that also includes freshly ground coffee.*

🍫 **FIELD NOTES** *While sweet white chocolate is not my favorite on its own, I happen to love the way it interacts with the bitter edge of coffee. This cookie is simple enough to make—just like any basic chocolate chip dough—but the chocolate-covered espresso beans and white chocolate elevate it to a sophisticated level. Try making half-size ones to serve alongside a shot of espresso.*

🍫 **LIFESPAN** *1 week at room temperature in airtight container*

Yield: *50 cookies*

♦ INGREDIENTS

2¼ cups all-purpose flour

1 teaspoon baking soda

1 teaspoon salt

1 cup (2 sticks) unsalted butter, softened

¾ cup granulated sugar

¾ cup firmly packed light brown sugar

2 tablespoons freshly ground dark roast coffee

1 teaspoon vanilla extract

2 large eggs

1½ cups white chocolate morsels

1 cup dark chocolate-covered espresso beans, roughly crushed

♦ DIRECTIONS

1. Whisk flour, baking soda, and salt together in a medium-size bowl.

2. In a large bowl with an electric mixer on medium-high speed, beat butter until creamy, about 2 minutes. Add granulated sugar and brown sugar gradually, beating until light and fluffy, about 3 minutes, and scraping down bowl once or twice. Beat in coffee and vanilla, then eggs, one at a time, scraping down bowl. Add about one-third of flour mixture and mix on low speed. Gradually add remaining flour mixture, mixing just until blended. Stir in white chocolate morsels and crushed espresso beans. Cover with plastic wrap and chill dough at least 2 hours or overnight.

3. Preheat oven to 375°F. Line 2 cookie sheets with parchment paper.

4. Drop chilled dough by generously rounded tablespoon 2 inches apart on prepared cookie sheets. Bake until edges and tops just begin to turn light golden brown, about 12 minutes. Place sheets on racks to cool for 5 minutes, then remove cookies from sheets and place directly on racks to cool completely.

Good Cookie Tip

Some chocolate-espresso candies are just shaped like coffee beans. For these cookies, make sure you get the real chocolate-covered espresso beans—there really is a coffee bean inside! They are what give this cookie its "kick." To crush, place them in a plastic bag and roll a rolling pin back and forth until they are roughly crushed. Some large pieces are not only okay, they are desirable. Also, I have made these with the addition of hazelnuts, pecans, or walnuts, and they are great!

Ginger Chip Brown Sugar Shortbread Fingers

🍫 **TYPE** *Molded cookie*

🍫 **DESCRIPTION** *Shortbread is a very buttery cookie and these live up to that expectation. These are made with brown sugar, crystallized ginger, and semisweet chocolate chips. You can use mini chocolate morsels right out of the bag or, for a more elegant look and taste, finely chopped bittersweet chocolate. Serve them up plain or dip one end in chocolate as suggested.*

🍫 **FIELD NOTES** *This shortbread cookie is patted into a pan, chilled, cut into finger-shaped cookies, then placed on a cookie sheet to bake. It is an easy way to mold the cookies so that they are even with nice square sides.*

🍫 **LIFESPAN** *2 weeks at room temperature in an airtight container if undipped; chocolate-dipped cookies may be stored for 3 days at room temperature in an airtight container in single layers separated by waxed (or parchment) paper*

Yield: *24 fingers*

🍫 INGREDIENTS

2½ cups all-purpose flour, sifted
1 cup (2 sticks) unsalted butter, softened
½ cup firmly packed light brown sugar
¼ teaspoon vanilla extract
¼ teaspoon ground ginger
¼ cup minced crystallized ginger

¼ cup miniature semisweet chocolate morsels or finely chopped bittersweet chocolate (about 1½ ounces)
7 ounces bittersweet or semisweet chocolate, finely chopped

🍫 DIRECTIONS

1. Coat a 9-inch square baking pan with nonstick cooking spray.

2. Whisk flour in a small bowl.

3. In a large bowl with an electric mixer on medium-high speed, beat butter until creamy, about 3 minutes. Add brown sugar gradually and beat on high speed until very light and fluffy. This may take as long as 8 minutes. Do not rush this stage; mixture should become very pale in color. Beat in vanilla and ground ginger. Add about one-third of flour and mix on low speed. Gradually add remaining flour, mixing just until blended and scraping down bowl once or twice. Before flour is completely incorporated, stir in crystallized ginger and morsels. Pat dough into prepared pan, making top as smooth as possible and pressing all the way to the sides and corners. Cover with plastic wrap and chill at least 2 hours or overnight.

4. Preheat oven to 325°F. Line a cookie sheet with parchment paper.

5. Cut shortbread into 24 bars (8 x 3). I find the best way to do this is with a stiff bench scraper. Use it to cut straight down, making even straight lines. Ease cookies out of the pan with a small metal spatula. They will be stiff and should come out cleanly. Place cookie fingers on prepared sheet evenly spaced. Bake until edges are just turning very light golden brown, about 30 minutes. Slide parchment onto rack to cool cookies completely.

6. Temper bittersweet chocolate as directed on page 14. Dip about 1 inch of the ends of cooled cookies into chocolate; allow excess chocolate to drip back into pot. Return cookies to parchment and place in refrigerator until chocolate is set.

Gloria's Beacon Hill Chocolate Chip Cookies

🍫 **TYPE** *Drop cookie*

🍫 **DESCRIPTION** *These are very chocolatey. They kind of look like meringues, as they are dry on the outside, but they are very moist and chewy on the inside!*

🍫 **FIELD NOTES** *There are many recipes for "Beacon Hill" cookies out there, but these are from Aunt Gloria. She is my partner's aunt and we had barely met when we started talking about chocolate. My kind of woman! The only change I made was to add chocolate morsels.*

🍫 **LIFESPAN** *4 days at room temperature in airtight container*

Yield: *45 cookies*

🍫 INGREDIENTS

6 ounces semisweet chocolate, finely chopped
2 large egg whites
½ cup granulated sugar
½ teaspoon vanilla extract

⅓ cup miniature semisweet chocolate morsels
⅓ cup walnut halves, toasted (see page 16) and finely chopped

🍫 DIRECTIONS

1. Preheat oven to 350°F. Line 2 cookie sheets with parchment paper.

2. Melt chopped chocolate in top of double boiler over gently simmering water or in a bowl in a microwave. Stir until smooth, then set aside to cool slightly.

3. In a large clean, grease-free bowl with an electric mixer on medium speed, beat egg whites until soft peaks form. Add sugar gradually and whip on high speed until stiff (but not dry) peaks form. Beat in vanilla, then fold in melted chocolate until combined; fold in chocolate morsels and walnuts. Drop by generously rounded teaspoon on prepared cookie sheets 2 inches apart.

4. Bake until crackled in appearance and dry on top, about 10 minutes; you should be able to lift cookies from pan. Insides should be very moist. Place sheets on racks to cool for 5 minutes, then slide parchment onto racks to cool cookies completely.

Half and Half Cookies

🍫 **TYPE** *Drop cookie*

🍫 **DESCRIPTION** *This recipe starts out with a basic chocolate chip recipe, but halfway through, you divide it and add cocoa and white morsels to part of the dough. Portions of the dark dough and light dough are baked together to give you a cookie that bakes up half as a regular chocolate chip cookie and half cocoa–white chocolate chip.*

🍫 **FIELD NOTES** *These look like they would be complicated to make, but they are not. The recipe is only a tad lengthier than one for standard chocolate chip dough. The cookies bake up remarkably evenly. They will each look a little different, which is okay. They will all taste great.*

🍫 **LIFESPAN** *1 week at room temperature in airtight container*

Yield: *52 cookies*

🍫 INGREDIENTS

2 cups plus 3 tablespoons all-purpose flour
1 teaspoon baking soda
1 teaspoon salt
1 cup (2 sticks) unsalted butter, softened
¾ cup granulated sugar
¾ cup firmly packed light brown sugar

1 teaspoon vanilla extract
2 large eggs
1 cup semisweet chocolate morsels
3 tablespoons Dutch-processed unsweetened cocoa powder, sifted
1 cup white chocolate morsels

🍫 DIRECTIONS

1. Whisk 2 cups of the flour, the baking soda, and salt together in a medium-size bowl.

2. In a large bowl with an electric mixer on medium-high speed, beat butter until creamy, about 2 minutes. Add granulated sugar and brown sugar gradually, beating until light and fluffy, about 3 minutes, and scraping down bowl once or twice. Beat in vanilla, then eggs, one at a time, scraping down bowl. Add about one-third of flour mixture and mix on low speed. Gradually add remaining flour mixture, mixing just until blended.

3. Divide mixture in half. To one half, beat in remaining 3 tablespoons flour and the semisweet chocolate morsels. To other half, beat in sifted cocoa and white chocolate morsels. Cover with plastic wrap and chill doughs separately at least 2 hours or overnight.

4. Preheat oven to 375°F. Line 2 cookie sheets with parchment paper.

5. Take a rounded teaspoon of each type of chilled dough and roll it into a ball. Press the balls together, side by side, so you can see both colored doughs. Gently form this cookie into a ball. Place on prepared cookie sheets 2 inches apart so that doughs remain side by side. Bake until edges and tops just begin to turn light golden brown, about 12 minutes. Place sheets on racks to cool for 5 minutes, then remove cookies from sheets and place directly on racks to cool completely.

Good Cookie Tip

Rolling both kinds of dough, then pressing them together, does take a little time. I like to first roll all of one flavor, then all of the other, then bring the two halves together one by one. Experiment to see what system works best for you. If you have kids around, get them involved!

Hazelnut Gianduja Chunk Cookies

🍫 **TYPE** *Drop cookie*

🍫 **DESCRIPTION** *These chocolate chip cookies combine the lovely pairing of hazelnuts and two kinds of chocolate. One is bittersweet, the other is called gianduja, which is a chocolate-hazelnut blend.*

🍫 **FIELD NOTES** *Gianduja, which is a mixture of hazelnuts and chocolate, can be made with either milk, semisweet, or bittersweet chocolate. The kind for this recipe is the milk chocolate type made by Callebaut. While it does contain hazelnuts, it looks like a chocolate bar and the texture is ultra smooth and creamy. Look for it at specialty food stores or purchase through mail order. The crunch in the cookies is provided by the added hazelnuts themselves.*

🍫 **LIFESPAN** *1 week at room temperature in airtight container*

Yield: *50 cookies*

INGREDIENTS

2¼ cups all-purpose flour
1 teaspoon baking soda
1 teaspoon salt
1 cup (2 sticks) unsalted butter, softened
¾ cup granulated sugar
¾ cup firmly packed light brown sugar
1 teaspoon vanilla extract

2 large eggs
1½ cups gianduja chocolate chunks
  (½-inch), about 7½ ounces
⅔ cup bittersweet chocolate chunks
  (½-inch), about 3½ ounces
⅔ cup hazelnuts, toasted (see page 15)
and chopped

DIRECTIONS

1. Whisk flour, baking soda, and salt together in a medium-size bowl.

2. In a large bowl with an electric mixer on medium-high speed, beat butter until creamy, about 2 minutes. Add granulated sugar and brown sugar gradually, beating until light and fluffy, about 3 minutes, and scraping down bowl once or twice. Beat in vanilla, then eggs, one at a time, scraping down bowl. Add about one-third of flour mixture and mix on low speed. Gradually add remaining flour mixture, mixing just until blended. Stir in chocolate chunks and nuts. Cover with plastic wrap and chill dough at least 2 hours or overnight.

3. Preheat oven to 375°F. Line 2 cookie sheets with parchment paper.

4. Drop chilled dough by generously rounded tablespoon 2 inches apart onto prepared cookie sheets. Bake until edges and tops just begin to turn light golden brown, about 12 minutes. Slide parchment onto racks to cool cookies completely.

Heavenly Hash Break-Up Bars

🍫 **TYPE** *Shaped cookie (sort of)*

🍫 **DESCRIPTION** *This chocolate cookie features black cocoa, which has a
very dark color and rich flavor. The dough is packed with white, milk, and semisweet
chocolate morsels, nuts, and marshmallows and is patted out onto a cookie sheet
in one large mass. After baking, the "cookie" is served by breaking off irregular hunks,
kind of like chocolate bark.*

🍫 **FIELD NOTES** *The departed Richard Sax left a legacy rich in delicious recipes
and I always find inspiration in his works. He wrote* The Cookie Lover's Cookie Book,
*and this recipe is based on one from that volume. The black cocoa can be ordered from
King Arthur Flour* The Baker's Catalogue *(see Resources).*

🍫 **LIFESPAN** *1 week at room temperature in airtight container in single layers
separated by waxed (or parchment) paper*

Yield: *20 large hunks of cookie*

🍫 INGREDIENTS

1 cup all-purpose flour
2 tablespoons unsweetened black cocoa
(see page 11) or Dutch-processed
unsweetened cocoa powder
½ teaspoon baking soda
¼ teaspoon salt
½ cup (1 stick) unsalted butter, softened
½ cup granulated sugar
¼ cup firmly packed light brown sugar

½ teaspoon vanilla extract
1 large egg
¾ cup semisweet chocolate morsels
½ cup white chocolate morsels
½ cup milk chocolate morsels
½ cup pecan halves, toasted (see page 16)
and chopped
1 cup miniature marshmallows

🍫 DIRECTIONS

1. Preheat oven to 350°F. Line a cookie
   sheet with parchment paper.

2. Sift flour, cocoa, baking soda, and salt
   together in a small bowl.

3. In a large bowl with an electric mixer
   on medium-high speed, beat butter
   until creamy, about 2 minutes. Add
   granulated sugar and brown sugar
   gradually, beating until light and fluffy,
   about 3 minutes, and scraping down
   bowl once or twice. Beat in vanilla,
   then egg. Add about one-third of flour
   mixture and mix on low speed.
   Gradually add remaining flour mixture,
   mixing just until blended. Stir in all
   chocolate morsels and nuts. Pat dough
   over cookie sheet as thin as possible,
   which will be about the width of a

chocolate morsel. If it is sticky, dampen
your palms. It is okay if dough mass is
not an even rectangle. It also might not
fill out the pan, which is just fine.

4. Bake until just dry to the touch, but a
   little soft inside, about 19 minutes.
   Remove from oven and scatter marshmallows all over top, as evenly spaced
   as possible. Carefully press the marshmallows into the dough, taking care as
   dough and the sheet are hot. Return
   sheet to oven and bake about 4 minutes more. Marshmallows should melt
   and create pockets of marshmallow
   and the dough should be fairly dry to
   the touch. Place sheet on rack to cool
   completely, then break into irregular-
   shaped pieces to serve.

Holy Smokes Heavenly Chip and Cranberry Cookies

🍫 **TYPE** *Drop cookie*

🍫 **DESCRIPTION** *This dough features moist dried cranberries and chunks of premium white chocolate baked up in a huge size—great for fall and winter holidays.*

🍫 **FIELD NOTES** *If you find yourself anywhere near Hatfield, Massachusetts, head for Holy Smokes BBQ & Whole Hog House, located in an 1888 church on Route 5. Proprietors Lou and Leslie Ekus, and son, Seth Crawford, serve these cookies warm from the oven, after you have gorged on some of the best ribs you have ever tasted.*

High-quality ingredients make a difference. I discovered a product called Paradise Meadow Sweetened Dried Premium Cape Cod Cranberries. They are larger and moister than any dried cranberries I have ever eaten, as well as being a gorgeous deep red color. You can mail-order them (see Resources). Lou and Leslie say make sure your white chocolate is high quality too.

🍫 **LIFESPAN** *1 week at room temperature in airtight container*

Yield: *20 cookies*

🍫 INGREDIENTS

2¾ cups all-purpose flour
I teaspoon baking soda
I teaspoon salt
I cup (2 sticks) unsalted butter, softened
¾ cup granulated sugar

¾ cup firmly packed light brown sugar
2 teaspoons vanilla extract
2 large eggs
2 cups white chocolate morsels
2 cups sweetened dried cranberries

🍫 DIRECTIONS

1. Preheat oven to 375°F. Line 2 cookie sheets with parchment paper.

2. Whisk flour, baking soda, and salt together in a medium-size bowl.

3. In a large bowl with an electric mixer on medium-high speed, beat butter until creamy, about 2 minutes. Add granulated sugar and light brown sugar gradually, beating until light and fluffy, about 3 minutes, and scraping down bowl once or twice. Beat in vanilla, then eggs, one at a time, scraping down bowl. Add about one-third of flour mixture and mix on low speed. Gradually add remaining flour mixture, mixing just until blended. Stir in chocolate morsels and cranberries. Drop by ¼-cup amounts 3 inches apart on prepared cookie sheets; do not flatten.

4. Bake until edges and tops just begin to turn light golden brown, about 15 minutes. Place sheets on racks to cool for 3 minutes, then slide parchment onto racks to cool cookies completely.

Lemon Espresso Chip Bars

🍫 **TYPE** *Bar cookie*

🍫 **DESCRIPTION** *You gotta love coffee to like these. They have a delightful bitter edge that comes from a shot of instant espresso. The lemon oil and candied lemon peel add another taste twist. These are not necessarily kid friendly. In fact, these can stand in for your afternoon coffee pick-me-up. They pack a caffeine wallop.*

🍫 **FIELD NOTES** *I used to sell these at my bakery, Harvest Moon, where they were quite popular. Many customers asked for the recipe and now, here it is.*

🍫 **LIFESPAN** *4 days at room temperature in airtight container*

Yield: *16 bars*

◢ INGREDIENTS

1 cup all-purpose flour
¾ teaspoon baking powder
¼ teaspoon salt
2½ ounces bittersweet chocolate, finely chopped
⅓ cup diced candied lemon peel
¾ cup (1½ sticks) unsalted butter, melted

¾ cup granulated sugar
¾ cup lightly packed light brown sugar
½ teaspoon vanilla extract
½ teaspoon lemon oil
  (see Good Cookie Tip)
3 large eggs
¼ cup instant espresso powder

◢ DIRECTIONS

1. Preheat oven to 325°F. Coat an 8-inch square baking pan with nonstick cooking spray.

2. Whisk flour, baking powder, and salt together in a small bowl. Add chopped chocolate and candied peel and toss to coat.

3. In a large bowl, whisk together melted butter, both sugars, vanilla, and lemon oil. Add eggs, one at a time, whisking well after each addition. Stir in instant espresso. Stir dry ingredients into butter-espresso mixture until just combined. Scrape into prepared pan and smooth top.

4. Bake until slightly puffed and edges have begun to pull away from sides of pan, about 55 minutes. A toothpick inserted in center should come out with some moist crumbs clinging. Place pan on rack to cool completely. Cut into 16 bars (4 x 4).

Good Cookie Tip

Lemon oil, made by Boyajian, can be ordered from Williams-Sonoma, or found at a local specialty food store. It is the distillation of oils from lemon zest and has an incomparable flavor. Do not substitute lemon extract. If necessary, try substituting finely grated zest from 1 lemon.

Magic Mini-Chip
Peanut Butter Kisses

🍫 **TYPE** *Drop cookie*

🍫 **DESCRIPTION** *The flavors of peanut butter, honey, and semisweet chocolate combine in this moist, easy-to-make cookie. These cookies will not spread, but retain their adorable "kiss" shape.*

🍫 **FIELD NOTES** *When I was in college, I came across a cookbook that had a recipe in it for a peanut butter cookie comprised simply of peanut butter, honey, and egg whites. I made them many times—absolutely loved them—and eventually the little paperback book fell apart and I lost the page. For years I searched for another copy to no avail and I failed at recreating the recipe. Then, as fate would have it, I met the daughter of the person who wrote the recipe at a culinary conference and through Jeanne Voltz's good graces the recipe came back to me. She and her mom share the same name, so at first I thought she was the originator. Her mom happened to be at the conference that year, so I got to meet her too. Thank you to both Jeannes!*
The only difference I have made is the addition of the mini-chips. They have given my version their blessing.

🍫 **LIFESPAN** *2 weeks at room temperature in airtight container in single layers separated by waxed (or parchment) paper*

Yield: *60 cookies*

🍫 INGREDIENTS

1 ½ cups smooth natural salted peanut butter (not hydrogenated like Skippy)

¾ cup honey

2 large egg whites

½ cup miniature semisweet chocolate morsels

🍫 DIRECTIONS

1. Preheat oven to 350°F. Line 2 cookie sheets with parchment paper.

2. In a large bowl with an electric mixer on medium speed, beat together peanut butter, honey, and egg whites until combined and smooth, about 2 minutes. Stir in chocolate morsels. Drop by generously rounded teaspoon 2 inches apart on prepared cookie sheets.

3. Bake until dry to the touch, about 10 minutes. If you gently lift a cookie, it will come off the parchment and the bottom will be just tinged with golden brown. Interior of cookie will be soft and will not have spread. Place sheets on racks to cool completely.

Good Cookie Tip

I am always specific when it comes to peanut butter. Some recipes, like this one, call for natural, non-hydrogenated peanut butter, and it is very important that you use that type. Other recipes work better with a hydrogenated type, and that will be specified in the recipe.

Melty Chocolate Chip Almond Toffee Bars

🍫 **TYPE** *Bar cookie*

🍫 **DESCRIPTION** *These are incredibly simple to make, but when you eat one, you might wonder "Where are the chips?" These begin with a shortbread-like crust. When they come out of the oven, semisweet chocolate morsels are sprinkled all over the top, and the chocolate then melts and can be spread all over the cookie for an instant chocolate frosting. Slivered almonds are sprinkled over the chocolate while it is still wet.*

🍫 **FIELD NOTES** *I have been making various "toffee bars" since I was a kid. They all start with a rich buttery base covered with chocolate, sometimes semisweet, sometimes milk chocolate, and then sprinkled with nuts, which can range from almonds to pecans. Their name always bothered me because, while the brown sugary cookie base is supposed to be toffee-like, I always thought it just tasted like a brown sugar cookie. But, since I figured folks would be looking for a "toffee bar" cookie in this book, I kept the name.*

🍫 **RELATED SPECIES** Melty Milk Chocolate Chip Pecan Toffee Bars: *Substitute milk chocolate morsels for the semisweet and toasted chopped pecans for the almonds.*

🍫 **LIFESPAN** *2 weeks at room temperature in airtight container in single layers separated by waxed (or parchment) paper or 3 weeks refrigerated in airtight container*

Yield: *24 bars*

◗ INGREDIENTS

2 cups all-purpose flour
¼ teaspoon salt
1 cup (2 sticks) unsalted butter, softened
1 cup firmly packed dark brown sugar
1 teaspoon vanilla extract
1 large egg yolk
1 cup semisweet chocolate morsels
1 cup slivered almonds, toasted
(see page 16)

Good Cookie Tip

Slivered almonds have a long, narrow, elegant shape, which I suggest for this cookie. Sometimes they can be hard to find, in which case you can substitute sliced almonds.

◗ DIRECTIONS

1. Preheat oven to 350°F. Coat a 9 x 13-inch baking pan with nonstick cooking spray.

2. Whisk flour and salt together in a medium-size bowl.

3. In a large bowl with an electric mixer on medium-high speed, beat butter until creamy, about 2 minutes. Add brown sugar gradually, beating until light and fluffy, about 3 minutes, and scraping down bowl once or twice. Beat in vanilla, then egg yolk. Add flour mixture gradually, mixing just until blended. Spread and pat evenly into prepared pan.

4. Bake until light golden brown, slightly puffed, and edges have begun to pull away from sides of pan, about 28 minutes. Place pan on rack and immediately sprinkle chocolate morsels evenly over top. Allow to sit until they soften, about 3 minutes. You have to touch them to tell; they will not melt. Use a small offset spatula to spread chocolate evenly over top, then immediately sprinkle almonds evenly over all. Let cool to room temperature, then place in refrigerator until chocolate firms and nuts adhere. Cut into 24 bars (6 x 4).

Ménage à Trois Cookies

🍫 TYPE *Drop cookie*

🍫 DESCRIPTION *These creamy, truffle-like dark chocolate cookies are best eaten within a day or two, when their texture is at their best. They are packed with white, milk, and bittersweet chocolate chunks, hence their name. These are the ultimate chocolate cookie and give you as much of a buzz as a small cup of coffee.*

🍫 FIELD NOTES *These are, indeed, a cookie version of a truffle. They are creamy, if at their best. This is why it is so important not to bake them too long. My friend Tom Bishop enthusiastically declared, "I have never had a chocolate chip cookie melt in my mouth!" That is as it should be with these!*

🍫 LIFESPAN *2 days at room temperature in airtight container in single layers separated by waxed (or parchment) paper*

Yield: *28 cookies*

🍫 INGREDIENTS

¼ cup all-purpose flour
¼ teaspoon baking powder
½ teaspoon salt
6 ounces semisweet chocolate, finely chopped
2 ounces unsweetened chocolate, finely chopped
6 tablespoons (¾ stick) unsalted butter, softened
¾ cup granulated sugar

2 large eggs
1½ teaspoons vanilla extract
2 cups semisweet or bittersweet chocolate chunks (½-inch), about 10 ounces
¾ cup milk chocolate chunks (½-inch), about 3¾ ounces
¾ cup white chocolate chunks (½-inch), about 3¾ ounces

🍫 DIRECTIONS

1. Preheat oven to 350°F. Line 2 cookie sheets with parchment paper.

2. Whisk flour, baking powder, and salt together in a small bowl.

3. Melt chopped semisweet and unsweetened chocolates and butter together in a medium-size saucepan over low heat or in a bowl in a microwave. Stir until smooth, then let cool slightly to a warm room temperature.

4. In a large bowl with an electric mixer, beat sugar, eggs and vanilla together on high speed until light and fluffy, 2 to 5 minutes. Gently fold in chocolate-butter mixture until no chocolate streaks remain. Fold flour mixture into batter until just combined.

5. Toss all the chocolate chunks together in a bowl; set aside about one-quarter of the mixture in another bowl. Fold the large portion of chunks into batter. Drop by generously rounded tablespoon 2 inches apart on prepared cookie sheets. Take reserved chocolate chunks and press at least one of each type onto each cookie top, so that they will show off the white–milk–dark chocolate trio when baked.

6. Bake until tops look and feel dry but insides are still soft and creamy, about 10 minutes. Edges will be slightly firmer than rest of cookie. They firm up tremendously upon cooling; do not overbake. Place sheets on racks to cool for 1 minute, then slide parchment onto racks to cool cookies completely. Make sure these cookies stay flat while cooling. They are delicate while warm.

Good Cookie Tip

These are delicate. Make sure to store them in single layers and keep the layers flat! They will keep longer than 2 days, but the texture will be less creamy and become more crumbly.

Milk Chocolate Butterfinger Brownies

🍫 **TYPE** *Bar cookie*

🍫 **DESCRIPTION** *This is a brownie made with melted milk chocolate added to the batter. Miniature semisweet chocolate chips and pieces of Butterfinger candy are folded in and decorate the top of each square. They are sweet, sweet, sweet, so get that sweet tooth ready!*

🍫 **FIELD NOTES** *I had never eaten a brownie made with milk chocolate in the batter, nor had I ever seen a recipe for one, so I figured it was high time to whip one up. I love peanuty, flaky, crunchy Butterfinger candy and thought it would go well with the milk chocolate brownie base.*

🍫 **LIFESPAN** *4 days at room temperature in airtight container in single layers separated by waxed (or parchment) paper*

Yield: *16 bars*

⬥ INGREDIENTS

1 cup all-purpose flour
Pinch of salt
½ cup (1 stick) unsalted butter, softened
4 ounces milk chocolate, finely chopped
½ cup sugar

2 large eggs
1 teaspoon vanilla extract
Four 2.1-ounce Butterfinger candy bars
½ cup miniature semisweet chocolate
   morsels

⬥ DIRECTIONS

1. Preheat oven to 350°F. Coat a 9-inch square baking pan with nonstick cooking spray.

2. Whisk flour and salt together in a small bowl.

3. Melt butter and chocolate together in a medium-size saucepan over low heat or in a bowl in a microwave. Stir until smooth and let cool slightly.

4. In a large bowl with an electric mixer on high speed, beat sugar, eggs, and vanilla together until light and fluffy, 2 to 5 minutes. Gently fold in chocolate-butter mixture until no chocolate streaks remain. Fold flour mixture into batter until just combined.

5. Take one of the candy bars and cut it into ½-inch pieces. Fold these and miniature chocolate morsels into batter and spread evenly in prepared pan. Cut remaining bars into 1½-inch pieces and press each one into the center of where each of the 16 bars will be; in other words, place them evenly four across and four down for a total of 16 pieces.

6. Bake until slightly puffed and edges have begun to pull away from sides of pan, about 30 minutes. A toothpick inserted in center should come out with some moist crumbs clinging. Place pan on rack to cool completely. Cut into 16 bars (4 x 4), centering pieces of candy for each bar.

Milk Chocolate Chip
Banana Streusel Cookies

🍫 **TYPE** *Drop cookie*

🍫 **DESCRIPTION** *These are soft cookies with mashed banana in the batter along with milk chocolate morsels. For added texture and flavor, they are topped with a brown sugar streusel packed with dried banana chips.*

🍫 **FIELD NOTES** *Make sure that your bananas are very ripe. There should be no green on the peel and they should have a few black speckles and be fragrant. For the best texture, just mash the banana with a fork in a small bowl; don't puree it.*

🍫 **LIFESPAN** *1 week at room temperature in airtight container in single layers separated by waxed (or parchment) paper*

☺

Yield: *24 cookies*

🍫 INGREDIENTS

Cookies:
1⅔ cups all-purpose flour
½ teaspoon baking soda
¼ teaspoon salt
½ cup (1 stick) unsalted butter, softened
¾ cup firmly packed light brown sugar
½ cup mashed ripe banana (from 1 small banana)
½ teaspoon vanilla extract
1 large egg
¼ cup buttermilk
1 cup milk chocolate morsels

Streusel:
½ cup crushed dried banana chips (sweetened or unsweetened)
¼ cup firmly packed light brown sugar
¼ cup walnut halves, toasted (see page 16) and finely chopped
¼ cup oats (use old-fashioned, not quick or instant)
2 tablespoons unsalted butter, melted
2 tablespoons all-purpose flour

🍫 DIRECTIONS

1. Whisk flour, baking soda, and salt together in a small bowl.

2. In a large bowl with an electric mixer on medium-high speed, beat butter until creamy, about 2 minutes. Add brown sugar gradually, beating until light and fluffy, about 3 minutes, and scraping down bowl once or twice. Beat in banana, then vanilla, then egg. Add flour mixture in thirds, alternating with the buttermilk. End with final addition of flour mixture, mixing just until blended. Stir in chocolate morsels. Cover with plastic wrap and chill dough at least 2 hours or overnight.

3. Preheat oven to 350°F. Line 2 cookie sheets with parchment paper. Make streusel while oven preheats. Combine streusel ingredients in a small bowl and stir to mix well.

4. Drop chilled dough by generously rounded tablespoon 2 inches apart on prepared cookie sheets. Sprinkle and press a bit of streusel on top of each cookie. Try not to get any around base of cookies. Bake until light golden brown, but still soft in the center, about 14 minutes. Place sheets on racks to cool cookies completely.

Good Cookie Tip

If you have a choice of buttermilks in your supermarket, choose lowfat as opposed to nonfat. The slightly richer flavor and texture works best, but you can substitute nonfat, if necessary. You could also use lowfat plain yogurt instead— or even banana-flavored yogurt!

Milk Chocolate Chunk Cookies with Grand Marnier and Pecans

🍫 **TYPE** *Drop cookie*

🍫 **DESCRIPTION** *These feature a classic brown sugar chocolate chip cookie dough with milk chocolate chunks, pecans, and the intriguing addition of candied orange peel and freshly grated orange zest. The shot of Grand Marnier is very nice, but orange juice can be used instead, if desired.*

🍫 **FIELD NOTES** *When The Black Sheep Deli and Bakery in Amherst, Massachusetts, opened its doors for the first time in February 1985, I was responsible for developing the recipes for and baking the cookies and brownies, among other sweets. These cookies were with us from day one and they are still being sold there.*

🍫 **LIFESPAN** *1 week at room temperature in airtight container*

Yield: *60 cookies*

● INGREDIENTS

2½ cups all-purpose flour
1 teaspoon baking soda
1 teaspoon salt
1 cup (2 sticks) unsalted butter, softened
1 cup firmly packed light brown sugar
½ cup granulated sugar
3 tablespoons Grand Marnier liqueur or
orange juice

2 teaspoons grated orange zest
1 teaspoon vanilla extract
2 large eggs
2 cups milk chocolate chunks (½-inch),
about 10 ounces
1 cup pecan halves, toasted (see page 16)
and chopped
¼ cup minced candied orange peel

● DIRECTIONS

1. Whisk flour, baking soda, and salt together in a medium-size bowl.

2. In a large bowl with an electric mixer on medium-high speed, beat butter until creamy, about 2 minutes. Add brown sugar and granulated sugar gradually, beating until light and fluffy, about 3 minutes, and scraping down bowl once or twice. Beat in 1 tablespoon of the Grand Marnier, the orange zest, and vanilla, then beat in eggs, one at a time, scraping down bowl. Add about one-third of flour mixture and mix on low speed. Gradually add remaining flour mixture, mixing just until blended. Stir in choco-late chunks, nuts, and candied peel. Cover with plastic wrap and chill dough at least 2 hours or overnight.

3. Preheat oven to 375°F. Line 2 cookie sheets with parchment paper.

4. Drop chilled dough by generously rounded tablespoon 2 inches apart on prepared cookie sheets. Bake until edges and tops just begin to turn light golden brown, about 11 minutes. Place sheets on racks to begin cooling. Brush cookie tops with remaining 2 table-spoons Grand Marnier and let cool 5 minutes more, then remove cookies from sheets and place directly on racks to cool completely.

Mocha Chip Cheesecake Brownies

🍫 **TYPE** *Bar cookie*

🍫 **DESCRIPTION** *These deep, dark, fudgy brownies are topped with a thick, creamy layer of coffee-flavored cheesecake studded with mini semisweet chocolate morsels. The beauty of these brownies is manyfold: they combine the luscious flavors of chocolate and coffee, they last for days in the refrigerator, and can even be frozen after baking with flawless results. They can be served in large squares to eat out of hand or be cut into small squares and presented in fluted paper cups.*

🍫 **FIELD NOTES** *New York–style cheesecakes continue to be an extremely popular American dessert. Cheesecake brownies appeared in force on the scene in the 1980s. I had a bakery at the time and while we had many variations, this is one of my favorites. When you see the term mocha, there is usually a combination of chocolate and coffee.*

🍫 **LIFESPAN** *1 week refrigerated in airtight container or frozen up to 1 month in single layers separated by waxed (or parchment) paper*

Yield: *20 bars*

🍫 INGREDIENTS

Brownies:
½ cup (1 stick) unsalted butter, softened, cut into tablespoons
8 ounces bittersweet or semisweet chocolate, finely chopped
½ cup granulated sugar
1 teaspoon vanilla extract
2 large eggs
½ cup all-purpose flour

Cheesecake:
One 8-ounce package cream cheese, softened
½ cup granulated sugar
2 teaspoons instant espresso or coffee
1 teaspoon vanilla extract
2 large eggs
2 tablespoons heavy cream
2 tablespoons all-purpose flour
¼ cup miniature semisweet chocolate morsels

🍫 DIRECTIONS

1. Preheat oven to 325°F. Coat a 9-inch square baking pan with nonstick cooking spray.

2. Melt butter and chocolate together in a medium-size saucepan over low heat or in a large bowl in a microwave. Once melted, whisk in sugar until smooth, then whisk in vanilla. Whisk in eggs, one at a time, mixing well after each addition, then stir in flour until combined and smooth. Scrape into prepared pan and smooth into an even layer.

3. In a medium-size bowl with an electric mixer on medium-high speed, beat cream cheese until creamy, about 2 minutes. Add sugar gradually and continue beating until light and fluffy, about 3 minutes, scraping down bowl once or twice. Whisk together instant coffee and vanilla, then beat into cream cheese mixture. Add eggs, one at a time, beating well after each addition and scraping down bowl. Beat in heavy cream and flour. Pour cream cheese mixture over brownie layer, spreading it evenly, then evenly sprinkle miniature chocolate morsels over top.

4. Bake until edges are light brown and beginning to pull away from edges of pan, about 45 minutes. Center should be set but still creamy. Place pan on rack to cool. Refrigerate overnight before cutting into 20 bars (4 x 5).

Good Cookie Tip

These are rich! I like to cut them into tiny 1½-inch squares. Place them in decorative fluted paper cups and offer them with coffee after dessert. In general, cutting cheesecake can be messy. Use a knife dipped in hot water and wipe it almost dry between cuts.

Mocha Walnut Chip Meringues

🍫 **TYPE** *Drop cookie*

🍫 **DESCRIPTION** *These are light and crispy and low in fat. They combine a simple meringue cookie containing powdered espresso with chopped walnuts and semisweet chocolate chips.*

🍫 **FIELD NOTES** *I went to Grace Church School in New York City for kindergarten through eighth grade and this recipe is based on one found in our church cookbook. They were called Surprise Meringues and didn't have the coffee added. The surprise is that you don't see the chocolate or nuts inside the cookies; they are the sweet surprise when you bite into one.*

🍫 **LIFESPAN** *2 weeks at room temperature in airtight container*

Yield: *45 cookies*

🍫 INGREDIENTS

2 large egg whites
⅛ teaspoon cream of tartar
¾ cup granulated sugar
1 tablespoon instant coffee or espresso
1 teaspoon vanilla extract
1 cup semisweet chocolate morsels
¼ cup walnut halves, toasted (see
    page 16) and finely chopped

Good Cookie Tip

After you chop the walnuts, place them in a strainer and shake over the sink to remove any powdery residue. You will be left with just firm, crunchy pieces of nuts and the texture of your cookies will be at their best.

🍫 DIRECTIONS

1. Preheat oven to 275°F. Line 2 cookie sheets with parchment paper.

2. In a large clean, grease-free bowl with an electric mixer on medium speed, whip egg whites until foamy. Add cream of tartar and whip until soft peaks form, increasing speed to medium-high. Add sugar gradually and whip on high speed until stiff, but not dry, peaks form. Stir instant coffee and vanilla together, then beat in. Fold in chocolate morsels and walnuts. Drop by generously rounded teaspoon on prepared cookie sheets 2 inches apart.

3. Bake until completely firm and dry, about 25 minutes; you should be able to lift cookies from sheet. Slide parchment onto racks to cool cookies completely.

Molasses Spice Chocolate Chip Cookies

🍫 **TYPE** *Drop cookie*

🍫 **DESCRIPTION** *The addition of molasses gives these cookies a chewy texture and rich, spicy flavor. The combo of molasses, spices, and chocolate might sound odd, but give it a try. Even my picky kids loved these.*

🍫 **FIELD NOTES** *Use unsulfured molasses for best flavor. Blackstrap is too strong.*

🍫 **LIFESPAN** *1 week at room temperature in airtight container in single layers separated by waxed (or parchment) paper*

Yield: *48 cookies*

🍫 INGREDIENTS

2¼ cups all-purpose flour
1 teaspoon baking soda
1 teaspoon salt
½ teaspoon ground cinnamon
½ teaspoon ground ginger
¼ teaspoon ground nutmeg
¼ teaspoon ground cloves

1 cup (2 sticks) unsalted butter, softened
1½ cups firmly packed dark brown sugar
¼ cup unsulfured molasses
1 teaspoon vanilla extract
2 large eggs
2 cups semisweet chocolate morsels

🍫 DIRECTIONS

1. Whisk flour, baking soda, salt, and spices together in a medium-size bowl.

2. In a large bowl with an electric mixer on medium-high speed, beat butter until creamy, about 2 minutes. Add brown sugar gradually, beating until light and fluffy, about 3 minutes, and scraping down bowl once or twice; beat in molasses until smooth. Beat in vanilla, then eggs, one at a time, scraping down bowl. Add about one-third of flour mixture and mix on low speed. Gradually add remaining flour mixture, mixing just until blended. Stir in chocolate morsels. Cover with plastic wrap and chill at least 2 hours or overnight.

3. Preheat oven to 375°F. Line 2 cookie sheets with parchment paper.

4. Drop chilled dough by generously rounded tablespoon 2 inches apart on prepared cookie sheets; flatten cookies, using your floured palm. Bake until edges and tops just begin to turn light golden brown (it is hard to see, so look carefully), about 11 minutes. Cookies will be a bit darker and firmer around edges, but soft on top. Place sheets on racks to cool for 5 minutes, then remove cookies from sheets and place directly on racks to cool completely.

Good Cookie Tip

These cookies are soft and can get sticky, so make sure to store them in single layers separated by waxed or parchment paper.

No-Bake Chocolate Chip Drops

🍫 **TYPE** *Drop cookie*

🍫 **DESCRIPTION** *This easy no-bake candy-like cookie is made with five ingredients and comes together in a flash. Semisweet and unsweetened chocolate are combined with sweetened condensed milk, white chocolate morsels, and nuts, then dropped by teaspoonfuls onto parchment paper.*

🍫 **FIELD NOTES** *Any kind of nut works here, so feel free to substitute pecans, walnuts, macadamias, almonds, pistachios, or peanuts.*

🍫 **LIFESPAN** *1 month refrigerated in airtight container in single layers separated by waxed (or parchment) paper; bring to room temperature before serving*

Yield: *45 drops*

▲ INGREDIENTS

6 ounces semisweet chocolate, finely chopped

2 ounces unsweetened chocolate, finely chopped

⅔ cup sweetened condensed milk

⅔ cup white chocolate morsels

½ cup chopped unsalted dry-roasted cashews

▲ DIRECTIONS

1. Line a cookie sheet with parchment paper; lightly coat with nonstick cooking spray.

2. Melt semisweet and unsweetened chocolates together in top of double boiler over gently simmering water or in a bowl in a microwave; stir until smooth. Stir in condensed milk until combined, then stir in morsels and nuts. Drop by generously rounded teaspoon ½ inch apart on prepared cookie sheet. Chill until firm, about 30 minutes. Serve at room temperature.

Oh So Minty, Oh So Chocolatey Creamy Dream Bars

🍫 **TYPE** *Bar cookie*

🍫 **DESCRIPTION** *These fudgy brownies have peppermint patties nestled in the middle for a very minty taste and creamy texture, hence the name.*

🍫 **FIELD NOTES** *These brownies were inspired by ones created by Maida Heatter. I have never seen a brownie like hers, which is baked at 475 degrees! I like to bake mine a little lower and slower, but the essence is the same. Because of the high heat, the edges might get a little crispy; if you don't like them, simply trim them off and discard.*

🍫 **LIFESPAN** *4 days at room temperature in airtight container in single layers separated by waxed (or parchment) paper*

Yield: *16 bars*

🍫 INGREDIENTS

¾ cup plus 2 tablespoons all-purpose flour

¼ teaspoon salt

4 ounces unsweetened chocolate, finely chopped

½ cup (1 stick) unsalted butter, softened

1¾ cups plus 2 tablespoons granulated sugar

3 large eggs

1 teaspoon vanilla extract

¾ cup miniature semisweet morsels

Seven 1.4-ounce (2½-inch-diameter) chocolate-covered peppermint patties

🍫 DIRECTIONS

1. Preheat oven to 400°F. Line an 8-inch square baking pan with aluminum foil so that it overhangs sides; you will be pulling the brownies out using this overhang. Coat foil with nonstick cooking spray.

2. Whisk flour and salt together in a small bowl.

3. Melt the chocolate and the butter together in a medium-size saucepan over low heat or in a bowl in a microwave. Stir until smooth, then set aside to cool slightly.

4. In a large bowl with an electric mixer on medium-high speed, beat sugar, eggs, and vanilla together until light and fluffy, about 3 minutes. Fold in cooled chocolate mixture, then fold in flour mixture and chocolate morsels.

5. Spread half of the batter into prepared pan. Place one round peppermint patty at each corner of pan and one in the center. Cut the other two in half crosswise and place the halves in the remaining spaces. Spread remaining batter evenly on top.

6. Bake until top is puffed, dry, and beginning to crack and edges have begun to pull away from sides of pan, about 25 minutes. A toothpick inserted in center should come out with some wet batter clinging. That's okay. Place pan on rack for 5 minutes to cool. Grasp the foil overhang and carefully pull brownies from pan. Place on rack to cool completely. I like to refrigerate these for several hours before cutting to firm them up (wrap them first in plastic wrap). Cut into 16 bars (4 x 4).

Good Cookie Tip

The folks at Reynolds have come out with nonstick aluminum foil called Release, which is perfect for this recipe and ones like it. If you use it, you won't need any nonstick spray.

Peanut Brittle Chip Bars

🍫 **TYPE** *Bar cookie*

🍫 **DESCRIPTION** *These candy-like bars feature a shortbread crust studded with miniature semisweet morsels and a honey-sweetened, crunchy peanut-brittle topping. Because I love chocolate, I have added a layer of semisweet ganache drizzled on top. P.S.: At room temperature these cookies are more cookie-like. Refrigerated, the caramel topping is solid, sticky, and like a peanut candy bar; I love them cold.*

🍫 **FIELD NOTES** *These are super sweet, but very popular. I use salted peanuts, which give the bar a salty-sweet quality that I really like. You can use unsalted, but try it this way first. To up the chocolate volume in this recipe, I added zigzags of chocolate over the peanut brittle; you may leave it off, if you like.*

🍫 **LIFESPAN** *1 week refrigerated in an airtight container, 4 days at room temperature*

Yield: *40 bars*

🍫 INGREDIENTS

Crust:
2½ cups all-purpose flour
¼ teaspoon salt
1 cup (2 sticks) unsalted butter, softened
½ cup granulated sugar
½ teaspoon vanilla extract
½ cup miniature semisweet chocolate
  morsels

Filling:
1 cup (2 sticks) unsalted butter, softened
1 cup firmly packed light brown sugar

1 cup honey
⅓ cup heavy cream
3 cups lightly salted dry-roasted peanuts,
  chopped
½ teaspoon vanilla extract

Topping:
5 ounces semisweet chocolate, finely
  chopped
2 tablespoons heavy cream

Good Cookie Tip

When shopping for ingredients for this recipe, I found reduced-salt peanuts, which I tried and really liked. They offered the perfect balance of salt in this sweet dessert.

🍫 DIRECTIONS

1. Coat a 9 x 13-inch baking pan with nonstick cooking spray.

2. Whisk flour and salt together in a medium-size bowl.

3. In a large bowl with an electric mixer on medium-high speed, beat butter until creamy, about 3 minutes. Add sugar gradually and beat on high speed until light and fluffy, scraping down bowl once or twice; mixture should be almost white in color. Beat in vanilla. Add about one-third of flour mixture and mix on low speed. Gradually add remaining flour, mixing just until blended and scraping down bowl once or twice. Stir in chocolate morsels, then pat crust in an even layer into prepared pan. Cover with plastic wrap and chill at least 30 minutes or overnight.

4. Preheat oven to 350°F, then bake chilled crust until just turning light golden brown around edges and top, but not fully cooked, about 25 minutes.

5. Prepare filling while crust is baking. Combine butter, brown sugar, and honey in a medium-size saucepan and cook over medium heat, stirring occasionally, until butter melts. Turn heat to high and bring to a boil. Reduce heat to medium-low and simmer 5 minutes. Remove from heat and stir in cream, peanuts, and vanilla. Pour filling over partially baked crust and bake until filling has darkened slightly, is bubbling all over, and edges have set, about 15 minutes. Place pan on rack to cool completely.

6. To make topping, melt chocolate and cream in a medium-size saucepan over low heat or in a bowl in a microwave. Stir until smooth. Place in a zipper-lock plastic bag, snip open one corner, and squeeze out topping making zigzags over completely cooled bars. Chill to set chocolate, about 10 minutes. Cut into 40 bars (5 x 8).

139

Peanut Butter Chocolate Chunk Cookies

🍫 **TYPE** *Drop cookie*

🍫 **DESCRIPTION** *These peanut butter cookies are packed with roasted peanuts as well as bittersweet chocolate chunks.*

🍫 **FIELD NOTES** *Use natural salted peanut butter for this recipe. I like Smucker's brand, which is nationally available and is consistent in texture. When you grind your own at the natural food store, it can really vary in oil content.*

🍫 **LIFESPAN** *2 weeks at room temperature in airtight container*

Yield: *30 cookies*

🍫 INGREDIENTS

1¼ cups all-purpose flour

½ teaspoon baking soda

¼ teaspoon salt

½ cup (1 stick) unsalted butter, softened

1¼ cups smooth, natural salted peanut butter (don't use hydrogenated like Skippy)

1 cup firmly packed light brown sugar

1 teaspoon vanilla extract

1 large egg

1 cup bittersweet chocolate chunks (½-inch), about 5 ounces

½ cup salted dry-roasted peanuts, chopped

🍫 DIRECTIONS

1. Whisk flour, baking soda, and salt together in a small bowl.

2. In a large bowl with an electric mixer on medium-high speed, beat butter until creamy, about 2 minutes. Add peanut butter and beat until smooth. Add brown sugar gradually, beating until light and fluffy, about 3 minutes, and scraping down bowl once or twice. Beat in vanilla, then egg. Add about one-third of flour mixture and mix on low speed. Gradually add remaining flour mixture, mixing just until blended. Stir in chocolate chunks and nuts. Cover with plastic wrap and chill dough at least 2 hours or overnight.

3. Preheat oven to 350°F. Line 2 cookie sheets with parchment paper.

4. Drop chilled dough by generously rounded tablespoon 2 inches apart onto prepared sheets. Flatten cookies with a fork, leaving tine marks. Bake until edges and tops just begin to turn light golden brown, about 15 minutes. Place sheets on racks to cool for 5 minutes, then remove cookies from sheets and place directly on racks to cool.

Peanut Butter Cup Chocolate Chip Cookies

TYPE *Drop cookie*

DESCRIPTION *If you love peanut butter cup candy, this cookie is for you. A peanut butter–enhanced chocolate chip cookie dough features the addition of chopped-up peanut butter cups and candy-coated peanut butter candies.*

FIELD NOTES *Like me, I am sure you think of Reese's Peanut Butter Cups and Reese's Pieces when it comes to peanut butter and chocolate candies. They are perfect for this recipe.*

LIFESPAN *1 week at room temperature in airtight container*

Yield: *54 cookies*

🍫 INGREDIENTS

2¼ cups all-purpose flour
1 teaspoon baking soda
1 teaspoon salt
1 cup (2 sticks) unsalted butter, softened
2 tablespoons smooth hydrogenated
  peanut butter (such as Skippy)
¾ cup granulated sugar
¾ cup firmly packed light brown sugar

1 teaspoon vanilla extract
2 large eggs
¾ cup semisweet chocolate morsels
⅔ cup Reese's Pieces peanut butter
  candies
Twelve .75-ounce Reese's Peanut Butter
  Cups, chopped (½-inch)

🍫 DIRECTIONS

1. Whisk flour, baking soda, and salt together in a medium-size bowl.

2. In a large bowl with an electric mixer on medium-high speed, beat butter and peanut butter together until creamy, about 2 minutes. Add granulated sugar and brown sugar gradually, beating until light and fluffy, about 3 minutes, and scraping down bowl once or twice. Beat in vanilla, then eggs, one at a time, scraping down bowl. Add about one-third of flour mixture and mix on low speed. Gradually add remaining flour mixture, mixing just until blended. Stir in chocolate morsels, candies, and peanut butter cup chunks. Cover with plastic wrap and chill dough at least 2 hours or overnight.

3. Preheat oven to 375°F. Line 2 cookie sheets with parchment paper.

4. Drop chilled dough by generously rounded tablespoon 2 inches apart on prepared cookie sheets. Bake until edges and tops just begin to turn light golden brown, about 10 minutes. Place sheets on racks to cool for 5 minutes, then remove cookies from sheets and place directly on racks to cool completely.

Piña Colada White Chocolate Chip Rum Bars

🍫 **TYPE** *Bar cookie*

🍫 **DESCRIPTION** *These very sweet bars are made from layers of crushed vanilla cookies, dried pineapple, coconut, rum, and macadamia nuts.*

🍫 **FIELD NOTES** *Sometimes it is hard to find unsalted macadamia nuts. For the purposes of this recipe, simply rub salted nuts vigorously between clean kitchen towels; it will remove enough salt.*

🍫 **LIFESPAN** *1 week at room temperature in an airtight container*

Yield: *30 bars*

🍫 INGREDIENTS

½ cup (1 stick) unsalted butter, cut into tablespoons

1½ cups vanilla cookie crumbs (made from about 60 Nabisco Nilla Wafers)

2 cups white chocolate morsels

1 cup sweetened flaked coconut

¾ cup chopped unsalted macadamia nuts

¾ cup diced sweetened dried pineapple

One 14-ounce can sweetened condensed milk

2 tablespoons dark rum

🍫 DIRECTIONS

1. Preheat oven to 350°F.

2. Place butter in a 9 x 13-inch baking pan; put pan in preheating oven to melt butter. Sprinkle cookie crumbs evenly over melted butter, stir with a spoon to combine, then pat crumbs into an even layer.

3. Place white chocolate morsels, coconut, nuts, and pineapple in a large bowl and toss to combine. The pineapple might be sticky; use your fingers to evenly combine mixture. In a small bowl, stir together condensed milk and rum. Sprinkle half the fruit-nut mixture evenly over crumb layer, then drizzle condensed milk and rum over all. Top with remaining fruit-nut mixture.

4. Bake until light golden brown around edges and beginning to turn light golden brown all over top, about 32 minutes. Middle will look a little loose; that's okay. Place pan on rack to cool completely. Cut into 30 bars (5 x 6).

Quick 'n' Easy One-Bowl Chocolate Chip Cookies

TYPE *Drop cookie*

DESCRIPTION *This is a basic chocolate chip cookie dough, in terms of ingredients. The technique is condensed so that you can make the dough in one bowl. If you have a microwave, the entire recipe can be completed in one bowl, making clean-up very easy. Otherwise, you have to melt the butter on the stovetop, then complete the recipe in a bowl.*

FIELD NOTES *Sometimes we want homemade chocolate chip cookies, but are short on time. This recipe is the answer. The cookies end up being very similar to the classic Toll House version.*

LIFESPAN *1 week at room temperature in airtight container*

Yield: *50 cookies*

INGREDIENTS

1 cup (2 sticks) unsalted butter, softened
¾ cup granulated sugar
¾ cup firmly packed light brown sugar
1 teaspoon vanilla extract
2 large eggs
2¼ cups all-purpose flour

1 teaspoon salt
1 teaspoon baking soda
2 cups plus 2 tablespoons semisweet chocolate morsels
1 cup walnut or pecan halves, toasted (see page 16) and chopped

DIRECTIONS

1. Preheat oven to 375°F. Line 2 cookie sheets with parchment paper.

2. Melt butter in a small saucepan over low heat or, preferably, in a large bowl in a microwave on medium power. When melted, whisk in both sugars until combined, then whisk in vanilla and eggs until completely combined. Allow to cool to room temperature. Add flour, salt, baking soda, chocolate morsels, and nuts and stir until well combined. Drop by generously rounded tablespoon 2 inches apart on prepared cookie sheets.

3. Bake until edges and tops just begin to turn light golden brown, about 10 minutes. Place sheets on racks to cool for 5 minutes, then remove cookies from sheets and place directly on racks to cool completely.

Good Cookie Tip

Allow the batter to cool before stirring in morsels or they will melt.

Rum Raisin
Chocolate Chunk Cookies

🍫 **TYPE** *Drop cookie*

🍫 **DESCRIPTION** *Rum-soaked raisins, walnuts, and semisweet chocolate chunks are added to a classic brown sugar dough.*

🍫 **FIELD NOTES** *You can use light or gold rum, but I love the rich flavor of gold. Because of the alcohol content, I consider these to be a grown-up chocolate chip cookie. They are very moist due to the addition of rum; make sure to bake them until light golden brown all over.*

🍫 **LIFESPAN** *1 week at room temperature in airtight container*

148

Yield: *50 cookies*

◆ INGREDIENTS

1 cup dark raisins
6 tablespoons gold rum
2⅓ cups all-purpose flour
1 teaspoon baking soda
1 teaspoon salt
1 cup (2 sticks) unsalted butter, softened
¾ cup granulated sugar

¾ cup firmly packed light brown sugar
½ teaspoon vanilla extract
2 large eggs
1¼ cups semisweet chocolate chunks
(⅓-inch), about 6¼ ounces
⅔ cup walnut halves, toasted (see page 16)
and chopped

◆ DIRECTIONS

1. Combine raisins and rum in a microwaveable bowl and heat on high power for 1 minute. Allow to sit for 15 minutes for rum to permeate the raisins. Alternatively, combine raisins and rum in a small saucepan, bring to a boil over medium heat, then remove from heat to soak while you prepare the dough. This plumps and flavors the raisins.

2. Whisk flour, baking soda, and salt together in a medium-size bowl.

3. In a large bowl with an electric mixer on medium-high speed, beat butter until creamy, about 2 minutes. Add granulated sugar and brown sugar gradually, beating until light and fluffy, about 3 minutes, scraping down bowl once or twice. Beat in vanilla, then eggs, one at a time, scraping down bowl. Add about one-third of flour mixture and mix on low speed. Gradually add remaining flour mixture, mixing just until blended. Drain raisins, reserving 1 teaspoon of the rum. Stir this rum into the dough along with the raisins, chocolate chunks, and

nuts. Cover with plastic wrap and chill dough at least 2 hours or overnight.

4. Preheat oven to 375°F. Line 2 cookie sheets with parchment paper.

5. Drop chilled dough by generously rounded tablespoon 2 inches apart on prepared cookie sheets. Bake until light golden brown all over, about 14 minutes. Place sheets on racks to cool cookies completely.

Good Cookie Tip

Use care if heating the raisins and rum on top of the stove. The rum can catch on fire if your flame is too high and comes over the top of the saucepan. Keep a low heat and you'll be fine.

Sour Cream Mini-Chip Cookies with Sour Cream Fudge Frosting

🍫 **TYPE** *Drop cookie*

🍫 **DESCRIPTION** *These soft cookies are enriched with sour cream and studded with mini-chips. To top it all off, they sport a swirl of thick sour cream fudge frosting. The tang of the sour cream in the frosting is addictively good.*

🍫 **FIELD NOTES** *The cookies, without frosting, will last at least 1 week. With frosting, they are best eaten the day they are made. Don't miss out on the frosting though. It is incredibly rich and fudgy—a must-have either on your cookies or straight off a spoon! In a larger quantity it also makes a great frosting for cake.*

🍫 **LIFESPAN** *1 week at room temperature in airtight container if unfrosted; eat same day if frosted*

Yield: *36 cookies*

🍫 INGREDIENTS

Cookies:
2 cups all-purpose flour
1 teaspoon baking soda
¼ teaspoon salt
½ cup (1 stick) unsalted butter, softened
1 cup granulated sugar
1 teaspoon vanilla extract
2 large eggs

½ cup sour cream
⅔ cup miniature semisweet chocolate morsels

Frosting:
5 ounces bittersweet or semisweet chocolate
½ cup sour cream

🍫 DIRECTIONS

1. Preheat oven to 350°F. Line 2 cookie sheets with parchment paper.

2. Whisk flour, baking soda, and salt together in a medium-size bowl.

3. In a large bowl with an electric mixer on medium-high speed, beat butter until creamy, about 2 minutes. Add sugar gradually, beating until light and fluffy, about 3 minutes, and scraping down bowl once or twice. Beat in vanilla, then eggs, one at a time, scraping down bowl. Add flour mixture in thirds, alternating with the sour cream. End with final addition of flour mixture, mixing just until blended. Batter will be thick. Stir in chocolate morsels. Drop by generously rounded tablespoon 2 inches apart on prepared cookie sheets.

4. Bake until edges just begin to turn light golden brown, about 12 minutes. Place on racks to cool for 5 minutes, then remove cookies from sheets and place directly on racks to cool completely.

5. To make frosting, melt chocolate in top of double boiler over gently simmering water or in a bowl in a microwave; stir until smooth. Let cool until slightly warm. (If it is too warm, it will melt the sour cream.) Fold in sour cream and keep stirring until frosting thickens to a creamy, spreadable consistency. Use immediately. If it is a little thin, let it sit for a few minutes; it will firm up to spreading consistency. It can sit for an hour, but do not refrigerate. Use an offset spatula to top each cookie with a generous swirl of frosting.

Sparkly Sunflower Cookies

🍫 **TYPE** *Rolled cookie*

🍫 **DESCRIPTION** *This sugar cookie dough is made with cream cheese, which gives it a richer taste and makes it very easy to work with. The dough is rolled out, then cut into sunflower shapes and covered with sparkly yellow sugar, with miniature chocolate chips used to form the center of the sunflower.*

🍫 **FIELD NOTES** *You can buy a sunflower-shaped cookie cutter from Sweet Celebrations (see Resources section). They make these cookies very realistic looking; or you could use any 3-inch petal-flower–shaped cutter. Note that your yield will vary depending on your particular cutter.*

🍫 **LIFESPAN** *2 weeks at room temperature in airtight container in single layers separated by waxed (or parchment) paper*

Yield: *twenty-five 3-inch sunflowers*

◆ INGREDIENTS

2½ cups all-purpose flour
1 cup (2 sticks) unsalted butter, softened
One 3-ounce package cream cheese, softened
1 cup granulated sugar

1 large egg yolk
1 teaspoon vanilla extract
½ cup miniature semisweet chocolate morsels
Yellow colored sugar

◆ DIRECTIONS

1. Whisk flour in a medium-size bowl.

2. In a large bowl with an electric mixer, beat butter on medium-high speed until creamy, about 3 minutes. Add cream cheese and beat until fluffy, about 2 minutes. Add sugar gradually and beat on high speed until very light and fluffy. Beat in egg yolk and vanilla. Add about one-third of flour and mix on low speed. Gradually add remaining flour, mixing just until blended and scraping down bowl once or twice. Cover with plastic wrap and chill dough until firm enough to roll, at least 30 minutes or overnight.

3. Line 2 cookie sheets with parchment paper.

4. Roll out chilled dough on lightly floured work surface to ¼-inch thickness. Cut out with sunflower-shaped cutter and place cookies 2 inches apart on prepared cookie sheets. Place chocolate morsels in middle of each cookie to make dark center of "sunflower." Depending on your cutter, this "center" will be about 1 inch in diameter. You can either cluster the morsels in a hodgepodge fashion or take the time to place them one by one so that each morsel is right side up. Sprinkle the petals (any exposed dough not covered with morsels) with yellow sugar to create a sparkly, colorful effect. Chill again on sheets while oven preheats. This helps keep their pretty shape.

5. Preheat oven to 350°F, then bake until completely firm and dry, about 14 minutes; you should be able to lift cookies from sheet. Slide parchment onto racks to cool cookies completely.

Surprise Chocolate-Filled
Heart Cookies

♦ TYPE *Rolled cookie*

♦ DESCRIPTION *This cream cheese cookie dough is very easy to roll out and work with. Here it's cut into heart shapes, then two hearts completely sandwich a small pile of chocolate chips flavored with brown sugar and cinnamon. That's the surprise! You can't see the filling until you bite into one.*

♦ FIELD NOTES *These are perfect for Valentine's Day, hence the dusting of pink and red sugar. If you like, they can be made with round cookie cutters and you can coat them with regular sugar. Or use shamrock cutters and green sugar for St. Patrick's Day, egg-shaped cutters and yellow and pink sugar for Easter…you get the idea.*

♦ LIFESPAN *1 week at room temperature in airtight container in single layers separated by waxed (or parchment) paper*

Yield: *twenty 2½-inch hearts*

♦ INGREDIENTS

Dough:
2½ cups all-purpose flour
1 cup (2 sticks) unsalted butter, softened
One 3-ounce package cream cheese, softened
1 cup granulated sugar
1 large egg yolk
1 teaspoon vanilla extract

Filling:
½ cup miniature semisweet chocolate morsels
1 tablespoon firmly packed light brown sugar
1 tablespoon jam, such as raspberry or apricot
¼ teaspoon ground cinnamon

Topping:
2 teaspoons heavy cream or milk
Red or pink colored sugar

♦ DIRECTIONS

1. Whisk flour in a medium-size bowl.

2. In a large bowl with an electric mixer on medium-high speed, beat butter until creamy, about 3 minutes. Add cream cheese and beat until fluffy, about 2 minutes. Add granulated sugar gradually and beat on high speed until very light and fluffy. Beat in egg yolk and vanilla. Add about one-third of flour and mix on low speed. Gradually add remaining flour, mixing just until blended and scraping down bowl once or twice. Cover with plastic wrap and chill dough until firm enough to roll, at least 30 minutes or overnight.

3. Make filling by stirring chocolate morsels, brown sugar, jam, and cinnamon together in a small bowl.

4. Line 2 cookie sheets with parchment paper.

5. Roll out chilled dough on lightly floured work surface to ⅛-inch thickness. Cut out 40 cookies with 2½-inch heart-shaped cookie cutter. Transfer 20 of these onto prepared cookie sheets. Place 1 teaspoon of filling in center of each heart and brush edges with water. Place another heart on top and press all the way around to seal and crimp with a fork. Brush tops with cream and dust with colored sugar of your choice. Chill again right on the sheets while oven preheats; this helps them keep their shape.

6. Preheat oven to 350°F.

7. Bake until just turning light golden brown around edges, about 16 minutes. Slide parchment onto racks to cool cookies completely.

Good Cookie Tip

Since you are sandwiching together two layers of dough, it is very important to roll it as thin as directed.

Triple Chocolate Chip Cookies in a Jar

🍫 **TYPE** *Drop cookie*

🍫 **DESCRIPTION** *This recipe is not for cookies per se, but actually for carefully and decoratively arranged ingredients. You layer colorful and distinct cookie ingredients in a jar, attach a note card, and give it as a gift—the gift of almost-instant cookies. This version, of which there are many, features three kinds of chocolate morsels. Success depends on making the layers of ingredients even and packing down each one as you go, or they won't fit in the jar!*

🍫 **FIELD NOTES** *My son's school made these as a fundraiser for their sixth-grade class trip, which is where I became familiar with them. I have seen many recipes for "cookies-in-a-jar," including oatmeal-raisin and brownie versions, both in magazine advertisements and on the Internet. I have no idea where the concept originated, but it is brilliant! You'll need a 1-quart widemouthed canning jar with a lid for this.*

Yield: *1 jar, 30 cookies*

🍫 INGREDIENTS

Cookies:
1¾ cups all-purpose flour
1 teaspoon baking soda
¼ teaspoon salt
¾ cup firmly packed light brown sugar
½ cup granulated sugar
¼ cup Dutch-processed unsweetened cocoa powder, sifted
½ cup semisweet chocolate morsels
½ cup milk chocolate morsels
½ cup white chocolate morsels

Decoration:
Note card
Hole-punch
One 8-inch square decorative fabric
Rubber band
24 inches of ½-inch ribbon

🍫 DIRECTIONS

1. Whisk flour, baking soda, and salt together in a small bowl.

2. Make sure jar is clean and completely dry. Pour flour mixture into jar and pack down firmly in an even layer using bottom of a small ladle or rubber spatula. Pour brown sugar into jar and tap down firmly (tapping down the brown sugar will help pack the flour layer beneath it). Follow with even layer of granulated sugar, then a layer of cocoa powder, again, packing down as you go. Wipe down sides of jar after cocoa is added, as some of it might cling. Add layer of semisweet morsels, following with layers of milk and white morsels. Tap down those ingredients. Screw top into place.

3. Make a hole in corner of note card with hole-punch. Write following directions on note card, along with any sentiments you might have for the receiver:

Triple Chocolate Chip Cookies in a Jar
Preheat oven to 350°F and line 2 cookie sheets with parchment paper. Melt 1½ sticks unsalted butter on stove or in large bowl in microwave; let cool. Whisk in 1 large egg and 1 teaspoon vanilla extract. Add contents of jar and stir until well combined; you might need to use your hands. Drop by generously rounded tablespoons 2 inches apart on prepared pans and press to flatten. Bake until the tops are cracked and dry, about 12 minutes; they will be soft on top and in the middle. Cookies will firm up upon cooling. Slide parchment onto racks to cool cookies completely. (Cookies may be stored at room temperature in an airtight container for up to 1 week.) Yields 30 cookies. Enjoy and Happy Baking!

4. Center fabric over top of jar and slip on rubber band to hold it in place just under the lid. Place ribbon over rubber band and tie ribbon by making the first step of tying a bow. Slip ribbon through hole in note card, then tie a bow.

Vanilla Mini-Chip Shortbread

🍫 **TYPE** *Rolled cookie*

🍫 **DESCRIPTION** *Shortbread is buttery and rich and usually contains only butter, sugar, and flour. Here I have added some vanilla extract and mini-chips for a chocolatey, chippy version. Shortbread keeps very, very well.*

🍫 **FIELD NOTES** *The "short" in shortbread refers to the fact that the dough itself is very "short," that is, loaded with shortening, in this case, butter.*

🍫 **LIFESPAN** *3 weeks at room temperature in airtight container*

Yield: *five 8-inch discs, each yielding 8 fans, for a total of 40 fans*

🍫 INGREDIENTS

5 cups all-purpose flour, sifted
1 cup miniature semisweet chocolate
morsels
2 cups (4 sticks) unsalted butter, softened

1 cup granulated sugar
1 teaspoon vanilla extract

🍫 DIRECTIONS

1. Line 3 rimless cookie sheets with parchment paper and sprinkle lightly with flour.

2. Whisk flour and chips together in a large bowl.

3. In another large bowl with an electric mixer on medium-high speed, beat butter until creamy, about 3 minutes. Add sugar gradually and beat on high speed until very light and fluffy. This may take as long as 8 minutes. Do not rush this stage; mixture should be almost white in color. Beat in vanilla. Add about one-third of flour mixture and mix on low speed. Gradually add remaining flour, mixing just until blended and scraping down bowl once or twice.

4. Divide the dough evenly into thirds. Roll each third out directly on prepared cookie sheet to ¼-inch thickness. Gently place an 8-inch cake pan over dough and cut out two 8-inch circles per sheet pan. Reroll any remaining dough. Crimp edges with a fork, like you would a piecrust, to create a rippled effect, if you like. Score 8 wedges into surface of dough using a small sharp knife. Prick shortbread all over with a fork or bamboo skewer either randomly or decoratively. Cover with plastic wrap and chill dough 2 hours or overnight.

5. Preheat oven to 325°F.

6. Bake until edges are just turning very light golden brown, about 30 minutes, but tops should remain as white as possible. Immediately cut into fan-shaped wedges while shortbread is still warm. This is best accomplished with a knife that is longer than the width of the shortbread; hold knife above the rounds and cut, pressing knife straight down, instead of dragging the tip through. Place sheets on racks to cool for a couple of minutes, then carefully remove wedges from sheets and place directly on racks to cool completely.

Walnut Espresso Rum Chip Butter Balls

🍫 **TYPE** *Shaped cookie*

🍫 **DESCRIPTION** *These cookies are easy to make in the food processor and combine ground walnuts, espresso, dark rum, sweet butter, powdered sugar, and vanilla for a buttery, crumbly, fancy cookie. You could use mini-chips, but in this cookie I prefer very finely chopped bittersweet chocolate.*

🍫 **FIELD NOTES** *The base for this cookie is similar to a pecan butter ball or Mexican wedding cake, but here I added the rum, coffee, and chocolate accents for a sophisticated cookie.*

🍫 **LIFESPAN** *2 weeks at room temperature in airtight container*

Yield: *56 balls*

🍫 INGREDIENTS

2 cups confectioners' sugar

2 tablespoons instant espresso powder

¾ cup walnut halves, toasted (see page 16) and chopped

¼ teaspoon salt

1 cup (2 sticks) unsalted butter, softened

2 teaspoons dark rum

½ teaspoon vanilla extract

2⅓ cups all-purpose flour

3 ounces bittersweet chocolate, finely chopped

🍫 DIRECTIONS

1. Place confectioners' sugar and instant espresso in a food processor and pulse until espresso is evenly dispersed. Remove 1½ cups of the mixture to a bowl. Add walnuts and salt to food processor and pulse to break up nuts, then process until nuts are finely ground. Add butter a few pieces at a time, pulsing to incorporate, then run machine until mixture is smooth; pulse in rum and vanilla. Add flour and chocolate and pulse until incorporated, scraping dough down once or twice. Process until dough begins to form a ball. Remove dough from machine, form into a very flat disc, cover completely with plastic wrap, and chill until firm enough to roll into balls, at least 2 hours or overnight.

2. Preheat oven to 350°F. Line 2 cookie sheets with parchment paper.

3. Roll chilled dough between your lightly floured palms into 1-inch balls and place on prepared cookie sheets 2 inches apart. Gently flatten just enough so they won't roll off sheet. Bake until light golden brown around edges, about 17 minutes. Set sheets on racks and let cool 5 minutes, then sift remaining 1½ cups confectioners' sugar mixture over warm cookies and roll them around for an even coating. After cookies have cooled, roll them in the sugar again to cover completely.

Good Cookie Tip

The idea is to cover these cookies completely with powdered sugar after they are baked. I usually roll them around in the confectioners' sugar several times. Make sure to coat them initially while still warm.

White Chocolate Bittersweet Chunk Brownies

🍫 **TYPE** *Bar cookie*

🍫 **DESCRIPTION** *Here white chocolate is melted and added to the brownie batter, making it particularly rich. Bittersweet chocolate chunks are folded in for a double chocolate brownie.*

🍫 **FIELD NOTES** *White chocolate is sweet, so make sure to use a bittersweet chocolate for the chunks in the batter. These look like a pretty mosaic when cut.*

🍫 **LIFESPAN** *1 week at room temperature in airtight container*

Yield: *16 bars*

🍫 INGREDIENTS

I cup all-purpose flour
Pinch of salt
½ cup (I stick) unsalted butter, softened
4 ounces white chocolate, finely chopped
½ cup granulated sugar

2 large eggs
I teaspoon vanilla extract
I cup bittersweet chocolate chunks
(½-inch), about 5 ounces

🍫 DIRECTIONS

1. Preheat oven to 350°F. Coat a 9-inch square baking pan with nonstick cooking spray.

2. Whisk flour and salt together in a small bowl.

3. Melt butter and white chocolate together in a medium-size saucepan over low heat or in a bowl in a microwave. Stir until smooth and let cool slightly.

4. In a large bowl with an electric mixer on high speed, beat together the sugar, eggs, and vanilla until light and fluffy, 2 to 5 minutes. Gently fold in butter–white chocolate mixture until no chocolate streaks remain. Fold flour mixture into batter until just combined; fold in chocolate chunks. Spread evenly in prepared pan.

5. Bake until edges begin to turn golden and pull away from sides of pan, about 32 minutes. A toothpick inserted in center should come out with some moist crumbs clinging. Place pan on rack until cool. Cut into 16 bars (4 x 4).

White Chocolate Chip Apricot Pistachio Cups

🍫 **TYPE** *Rolled and molded cookie*

🍫 **DESCRIPTION** *These tiny pastry-like cookies are formed in mini-muffin tins. The rich cream cheese pastry crust is not sweet and encases a lovely, sophisticated filling of chopped apricots, pistachios, and white chocolate morsels.*

🍫 **FIELD NOTES** *These are elegant and would be perfect for an afternoon tea or a shower party.*

🍫 **LIFESPAN** *1 week at room temperature in an airtight container*

Yield: *48 cookies*

🍫 INGREDIENTS

Dough:

1½ cups all-purpose flour

4 ounces chilled cream cheese (half an 8-ounce package), cut into tablespoons

½ cup (1 stick) chilled unsalted butter, cut into tablespoons

Filling:

2 large eggs, separated

½ cup (1 stick) unsalted butter, softened

1 cup granulated sugar

1 teaspoon vanilla extract

⅓ cup dried apricots, finely chopped

⅓ cup shelled unsalted natural pistachios, finely chopped

¼ cup finely chopped white chocolate (about ⅛-inch with some slivers), about 1½ ounces

Confectioners' sugar (optional)

🍫 DIRECTIONS

1. To make dough, place flour in a food processor and pulse to aerate. With machine running, add cream cheese and butter a few pieces at a time through feed tube and process until evenly combined and dough begins to form moist clumps. Remove dough from machine, wrap in plastic wrap, and chill at least 2 hours or up to 2 days.

2. To make filling, in a medium-size clean, grease-free bowl with an electric mixer on medium-high speed, whip egg whites until soft peaks form. In a separate large bowl with the mixer on medium-high speed, beat butter until creamy, about 3 minutes. Add granulated sugar gradually and continue beating until light and fluffy, about 5 minutes, scraping down bowl once or twice. Beat in vanilla. Add egg yolks, one at a time, beating well after each addition and scraping down bowl. Fold in beaten egg whites, apricots, pistachios, and white chocolate until evenly combined.

3. Preheat oven to 375°F. Coat four 12-cup mini-muffin tins with nonstick cooking spray.

4. Roll chilled dough out to ¼-inch thickness on lightly floured work surface. Cut out circles using a 2½-inch round cookie cutter (fluted or straight edged). Press rounds into each muffin well and smooth out bottom and sides. Fill with about 1 teaspoon of filling; it should come about three-quarters of the way up the sides; do not overfill. Bake until light golden brown all over top and slightly darker brown around edges, about 16 minutes.

5. Place tins on racks for a couple of minutes, then unmold cups and place directly on racks to cool completely. To help remove from tins, insert the tip of a butter knife between the cookie and the tin and gently apply inward and upward pressure to release it. Dust tops with confectioners' sugar right before serving, if desired.

White Chocolate Chip Lemon Pucker Cookies

🍫 **TYPE** *Shaped cookie*

🍫 **DESCRIPTION** *These are very sour lemony cookies. They feature lemon oil, lemon zest, and—the secret ingredient—citric acid. This comes in powder form and coats the cookies along with powdered sugar and yellow colored sugar (for that lemon look). If you are a fan of sour candies, then these are for you; citric acid coats those as well. You can also use less of the citric acid if you like, but these cookies are meant to be sour, sour, sour.*

🍫 **FIELD NOTES** *Most likely you will have to special order the citric acid. It might sound scary but it's not; it's what makes all those sour candies so puckery. I figured, why not on a cookie? The lemon oil can be found in specialty stores or mail-ordered; see Resources.*

🍫 **LIFESPAN** *2 weeks at room temperature in airtight container*

Yield: *56 cookies*

🍫 INGREDIENTS

Cookies:
2 cups all-purpose flour
⅔ cup blanched whole almonds
Heaping ½ cup white chocolate morsels
Pinch of salt
¾ cup confectioners' sugar
1 cup (2 sticks) unsalted butter, softened
1 tablespoon grated lemon zest

1 teaspoon lemon oil (don't substitute lemon extract)
1 large egg yolk

Topping:
½ cup yellow colored sugar
½ cup confectioners' sugar
1 tablespoon plus 1 teaspoon citric acid

🍫 DIRECTIONS

1. Place flour, almonds, ¼ cup of the white chocolate morsels, and the salt in a food processor and pulse to coarsely chop nuts and chocolate, then turn machine on and process until finely ground. Pulse in confectioners' sugar.

2. With machine running, add butter in pieces through feed tube until incorporated. Pulse in lemon zest, lemon oil, and egg yolk, then process until dough comes together and forms a ball. Cover dough completely with plastic wrap and chill until firm enough to roll, at least 2 hours or overnight, in which case you may need it to soften a bit at room temperature before shaping.

3. Preheat oven to 350°F. Line 2 cookie sheets with parchment paper. While oven preheats, stir together topping ingredients in a small bowl.

4. Roll chilled dough between your palms into 1-inch balls. Using remaining heaping ¼ cup white chocolate morsels, press 2 morsels deep inside each ball, enclosing them completely with dough. Place cookies on prepared cookie sheets about 2 inches apart and gently flatten just enough so they won't roll off. Bake until light golden brown around edges and on bottoms, about 17 minutes. Slide parchment onto racks to cool for a minute or two.

5. While still warm, roll each cookie in topping mixture until completely covered; you might have to roll them around a few times. Return to parchment on rack to cool completely.

White Chocolate Chunk Cookies with Macadamias

🍫 **TYPE** *Drop cookie*

🍫 **DESCRIPTION** *This recipe takes a classic brown sugar dough and adds white chocolate and chopped buttery macadamia nuts for a tasty, and now very common, variation.*

🍫 **FIELD NOTES** *It seems as though bakers are constantly coming up with "new" versions of the chocolate chip cookie. I don't know who developed this one originally— some say it was Mrs. Fields—but it is now found far and wide, in bakeries and even in bags in the cookie aisle of the supermarket. Now you can make my version at home.*

🍫 **LIFESPAN** *1 week at room temperature in airtight container*

Yield: *50 cookies*

🍫 INGREDIENTS

2¼ cups all-purpose flour
1 teaspoon baking soda
1 teaspoon salt
1 cup (2 sticks) unsalted butter, softened
¾ cup granulated sugar
¾ cup firmly packed light brown sugar

1 teaspoon vanilla extract
2 large eggs
2¼ cups white chocolate chunks (½-inch),
about 11¼ ounces
¾ cup macadamias, toasted (see page 16)
and chopped

🍫 DIRECTIONS

1. Whisk flour, baking soda, and salt together in a medium-size bowl.

2. In a large bowl with an electric mixer on medium-high speed, beat butter until creamy, about 2 minutes. Add granulated sugar and brown sugar gradually, beating until light and fluffy, about 3 minutes, and scraping down bowl once or twice. Beat in vanilla, then eggs, one at a time, scraping down bowl. Add about one-third of flour mixture and mix on low speed. Gradually add remaining flour mixture, mixing just until blended. Stir in chocolate chunks and nuts. Cover with plastic wrap and chill dough at least 2 hours or overnight.

3. Preheat oven to 375°F. Line 2 cookie sheets with parchment paper.

4. Drop chilled dough by generously rounded tablespoon 2 inches apart on prepared cookie sheets. Bake until edges and tops just begin to turn light golden brown, about 12 minutes. Place sheets on racks to cool for 5 minutes, then remove cookies from sheets and place directly on racks to cool completely.

White Pearl Chocolate Chip Brownie Drops

🍫 **TYPE** *Drop cookie*

🍫 **DESCRIPTION** *These dark chocolate brownie-like cookies have white chocolate morsels nestled inside—they look like pearls!*

🍫 **FIELD NOTES** *These are kind of reverse chocolate chip cookies with cocoa in the dough and white chips instead of dark. You can find white chips everywhere these days. Usually I think white chocolate is a little too sweet, but with the cocoa-enhanced dough, they have found a happy home.*

🍫 **LIFESPAN** *4 days at room temperature in airtight container in single layers separated by waxed (or parchment) paper*

Yield: *52 cookies*

◢ INGREDIENTS

2¼ cups all-purpose flour
⅔ cup Dutch-processed unsweetened
  cocoa powder
1 teaspoon baking soda
1 teaspoon salt
1½ cups (3 sticks) unsalted butter,
  softened

1 cup granulated sugar
⅔ cup firmly packed light brown sugar
1 teaspoon vanilla extract
2 large eggs
2 cups white chocolate morsels

◢ DIRECTIONS

1. Sift flour, cocoa, baking soda, and salt together in a medium-size bowl.

2. In a large bowl with an electric mixer on medium-high speed, beat butter until creamy, about 2 minutes. Add granulated sugar and brown sugar gradually, beating until light and fluffy, about 3 minutes, and scraping down bowl once or twice. Beat in vanilla, then eggs, one at a time, scraping down bowl. Add about one-third of flour mixture and mix on low speed. Gradually add remaining flour mixture, mixing just until blended. Stir in chocolate morsels. Cover with plastic wrap and chill dough at least 2 hours or overnight.

3. Preheat oven to 350°F. Line 2 cookie sheets with parchment paper.

4. Drop chilled dough by generously rounded tablespoon 2 inches apart on prepared cookie sheets. Bake until dry to touch but still a bit soft, about 11 minutes. Place sheets on racks and let cookies cool completely.

Resources

Beryl's Cake Decorating and Pastry Supplies
P.O. Box 1584
North Springfield, VA 22151
(703) 256-6951
(800) 488-2749
FAX (703) 750-3779
www.beryls.com
There is a Beryl, who will often answer the phone herself. This is one of my first stops for bakery supplies. She provides highly personal and professional customer service and her company supplies cutters and pans of all shapes and sizes, books, and more. Print catalog available, as is a CD-Rom.

Blue Magic
The Luce Corporation
336 Putnam Avenue
P.O. Box 4124
Hamden, CT 06514
(203) 787-0281
Blue Magic moisture absorbers are small devices a little larger than a walnut that have a clear glass bottom and perforated metal top. Inside is a dry chemical that absorbs moisture. You place one of these devices in your cookie jar and it absorbs any moisture so that crisp cookies stay crisp. It's called "blue" magic because the chemical changes from blue to pinkish-white as it absorbs moisture. When it has completely turned pinkish-white, you just dry it out in the oven or toaster oven and when it's blue again, it's ready to use once more. You can buy the small units by themselves to place in your own containers or you can buy canisters that have the Blue Magic unit built in. Call for catalog and order form.

Cape Cod Provisions
55 Jonathan Bourne Drive
Pocasset, MA 02559
(888) 811-2379
This company will mail you 6-ounce retail packs of the moistest, most delicious dried cranberries you have ever tasted. Just ask for the Paradise Meadow cranberries; you will be glad you made the effort for your cookies.

The Chef's Catalog
3215 Commercial Avenue
Northbrook, IL 60062-1900
(800) 338-3232
www.chefscatalog.com
This is a great mail-order catalog with very competitive prices. You'll find KitchenAid mixers, large professional-sized rubber spatulas, extra-long hot-mitts, parchment paper, and more. Catalog available.

Chocosphere
(877) 99CHOCO
FAX (877) 992-4626
www.chocosphere.com
If you are looking for high-quality chocolate, make this your first stop. This company specializes in all my favorite chocolates that are great to eat and to use in your baked goods, whether melted or cut into chunks. Owner Jerry Kryszek offers excellent personal service and they ship nationwide. Either order through the Web site or call to place your order.

King Arthur Flour
The Baker's Catalogue
P.O. Box 876
Norwich, VT 05055
(800) 827-6836
FAX (802) 649-5359
www.kingarthurflour.com
This catalog, which is updated often, offers high-quality flours, extracts, chocolates, candied fruit and citrus rinds, scales, and high-quality measuring cups, including ones in odd sizes. They have small ice cream scoops that make baking cookies quick and easy; ask for the Zeroll brand in the "teaspoon" and "tablespoon" sizes. The #100 size corresponds to a generous teaspoon and the #40 size dishes up a generous tablespoon. They also have terracotta discs that can be soaked in water and added to jars of soft cookies to help them stay nice and moist. Catalog available.

KitchenAid
P.O. Box 218
St. Joseph, MI 49085
(800) 541-6390
www.kitchenaid.com
Go directly to this Web site for a complete listing of their high-quality products. All of my cookies were tested in a KitchenAid oven and made with a KitchenAid mixer. I bought my mixer almost

20 years ago and it is still going strong; this is a worthwhile investment for any avid baker.

New York Cake and Baking Distributors
56 West 22nd Street
New York, NY 10010
(212) 675-2253
(800) 942-2539
www.nycakesupplies.com
You can shop here for a huge variety of colored sugars in many textures, food coloring, cookie sheets, parchment paper, cookie cutters, high-quality chocolates, and more.

Penzeys Spices
P.O. Box 993
W19362 Apollo Drive
Muskego, WI 53150
(800) 741-7787
FAX (262) 785-7678
www.penzeys.com
This company has an amazing array of fresh herbs and spices. Check them out for excellent cinnamon, nutmeg, ginger, and vanilla extract, among other ingredients. Catalog available.

Sur La Table
Pike Place Farmers' Market
84 Pine Street
Seattle, WA 98101
(206) 448-2244
(800) 243-0852
www.surlatable.com
Here you will find rolling pins, high-quality cookie-sheet pans, spatulas, and more. Catalog available.

Sweet Celebrations/ Maid of Scandinavia
7009 Washington Avenue South
Edina, MN 55439
(800) 328-6722
www.sweetc.com
www.maidofscandinavia.com
This company used to be called Maid of Scandinavia, but is now called Sweet Celebrations. They offer a huge array of equipment and ingredients, such as Scharffen Berger Cacao Nibs and terra-cotta discs that will help keep soft cookies soft. They also have an amazing array of cookie cutters. Catalog available.

Williams-Sonoma
P.O. Box 7456
San Francisco, CA 94120
(415) 421-4242
(800) 541-2233
FAX (415) 421-5253
www.williams-sonoma.com
Famous for their mail-order catalog, they also have stores nationwide. You will find well-made accurate measuring tools, KitchenAid mixers, vanilla extract, some chocolate and cocoa, and other baking equipment, including pans and spatulas of all sorts.

Wilton Industries, Inc.
2240 West 75th Street
Woodbridge, IL 60517
(708) 963-7100
(800) 794-5866
www.wilton.com
Great catalog with heavy-duty pans, food coloring, cookie cutters, parchment paper, chocolates, cocoa, and much more.

Measurement Equivalents

Please note that all conversions are approximate.

Liquid Conversions

U.S.	Metric
1 tsp	5 ml
1 tbs	15 ml
2 tbs	30 ml
3 tbs	45 ml
¼ cup	60 ml
⅓ cup	75 ml
⅓ cup + 1 tbs	90 ml
⅓ cup + 2 tbs	100 ml
½ cup	120 ml
⅔ cup	150 ml
¾ cup	180 ml
¾ cup + 2 tbs	200 ml
1 cup	240 ml
1 cup + 2 tbs	275 ml
1¼ cups	300 ml
1⅓ cups	325 ml
1½ cups	350 ml
1⅔ cups	375 ml
1¾ cups	400 ml
1¾ cups + 2 tbs	450 ml
2 cups (1 pint)	475 ml
2½ cups	600 ml
3 cups	720 ml
4 cups (1 quart)	945 ml (1,000 ml is 1 liter)

Weight Conversions

U.S./U.K.	Metric
½ oz	14 g
1 oz	28 g
1½ oz	48 g
2 oz	57 g
2½ oz	66 g
3 oz	85 g
3½ oz	100 g
4 oz	113 g
5 oz	142 g
6 oz	170 g
7 oz	200 g
8 oz	227 g
9 oz	255 g
10 oz	284 g
11 oz	312 g
12 oz	340 g
13 oz	368 g
14 oz	400 g
15 oz	425 g
1 lb	454 g

Oven Temperature Conversions

°F	Gas Mark	°C
250	½	120
275	1	140
300	2	150
325	3	165
350	4	180
375	5	190
400	6	200
425	7	220
450	8	230
475	9	240
500	10	260
550	Broil	290

Index